Not
the
Type

Born and educated in Scotland, **Camilla Thurlow** attended university in England, and left with a First, determined to try to do something that would make a difference, rather than set about a more traditional career. At the age of twenty-three she was accepted by The HALO Trust to train in explosive ordnance disposal – finding and clearing landmines in some of the world's most dangerous and inhospitable places, including Afghanistan, Zimbabwe, Mozambique and Cambodia. Seeking a new challenge, she was invited and was accepted to appear as a contestant on *Love Island*, and came second in the 2017 series – an experience she said she found far more nerve-racking than clearing landmines. She lives in East Anglia with her partner, Jamie Jewitt – whom she met on *Love Island* – and their first child, a daughter born in October 2020.

Not the Type

Finding your place
in the real world

Camilla Thurlow

metro

First published in the UK by Metro Publishing,
an imprint of John Blake Publishing.
An imprint of Bonnier Books UK
80–81 Wimpole Street, London, W1G 9RE
Owned by Bonnier Books
Sveavägen 56, Stockholm, Sweden

www.facebook.com/johnblakebooks
twitter.com/jblakebooks

First published in hardback in 2020
Paperback edition first published in 2021

Paperback ISBN: 978-1-78946-409-2
Hardback ISBN: 978-1-78946-343-9
Signed hardback ISBN: 978-1-78946-367-5
Ebook ISBN: 978-1-978-1-78946-345-3
Audio book ISBN: 978-1-78946-309-5

British Library Cataloguing-in-Publication Data:

A catalogue record for this book is available from the British Library.

Design by www.envydesign.co.uk

Printed and bound in Great Britain by Clays Ltd, Elcograf S.p.A

1 3 5 7 9 10 8 6 4 2

Every reasonable effort has been made to trace copyright-holders of material
reproduced in this book, but if any have been inadvertently overlooked the publishers
would be glad to hear from them.

John Blake Publishing is an imprint of Bonnier Books UK
www.bonnierbooks.co.uk

For Chris and Erica

Note: The names of some individuals have been changed to protect their privacy.

Contents

Introduction

I was dozing off, my hands loosely clutching a cheap copy of a fashionable Motorola flip phone in my lap. The roads were familiar even in the middle of the night. I had been driven along this route many times journeying between school and home. We had reached the Dalveen Pass, a deep valley in the Lowther Hills that lie midway along the road between Dumfries, my hometown, and Edinburgh, where my school was, some seventy miles to the north-east.

I was returning from a training weekend for the upcoming U19 Lacrosse World Championships, and had been picked up after landing at Edinburgh Airport at about 1 a.m. In a moment that I remember with startling clarity, the car clipped the verge on the left and then spun, sending us over the edge and down into the steep valley. The car continued to somersault, with our heads smacking against the dashboard and then back against the headrest, before coming to a stop upside-down.

The impact had forced the offside door outwards, and the driver was able to climb out and back up the valley, to get a signal to call the emergency services, but the passenger side had buckled inwards, trapping me. I was hanging upside-down from the seatbelt cutting into my middle, with my head pressing on a shard of glass from the sunroof that had been smashed upward and stabbed into my scalp. When the emergency services eventually got to us, they cut away my door and lifted me clear, then strapped me on a pulley stretcher and hauled me up the valley to the road. Amazingly, apart from the cut on my head, whiplash, and a very sore stomach from where the seatbelt had cut into me, I was completely fine. At the hospital I was given some strong painkillers to take over the coming weeks, but one of the drugs was on the banned list we had been given, so I couldn't take it. As a result, training was uncomfortable, though not impossible, and I went on to compete in the championships alongside my teammates.

I remember the police coming to speak to us in the days that followed, telling us how lucky we had been. How, when they saw the state of the vehicle, crushed and broken at the bottom of the valley, they had been expecting fatalities, rather than just the two of us, a bit shaken but largely uninjured.

Up until that point, I don't think I had realised how lucky a person I was. The crash ruptured the safe little bubble I believed I lived in. It was also instrumental in my coming to understand how much of life is down to chance and luck.

I'm now an exceptionally nervous driver. It took me four attempts to pass my driving test, and I did everything to get through it, even taking the third in a nearby village that had a higher pass rate – and I still failed. I am constantly, if affectionately, mocked by Jamie for my frantic apologies to all other road users because of my persistent indecisiveness. If I have to switch lanes, I will spend minutes leaning out the window mouthing apologies at the nearest cars. He now finds it hilarious to stick his arm out the window and put up his middle finger, while saying to me, 'If you're going to do something wrong, at least make it seem like you meant to!'

It's odd, in a way, that I dislike driving so much, for it plays into so many of my desires: my need to be independent; to travel; to leave. But there is still a part of me that believes the worst will happen, that doesn't trust myself to do as I've been taught. The only way I can explain this is to compare it to the feeling you get at the top of a very high building, and it feels almost as though you might just step out and over the edge – even though in reality you won't. It's just an odd feeling, like your mind is testing your body to see how much influence it can exert over it. Whenever I drive, I feel like I might do something stupid, that I might misjudge something, and because I have known it to happen before, it is very hard to convince myself otherwise. I don't have nightmares about the accident, as I was warned I might. Instead, I revisit it in my daily life, in the context in which it is most relevant, so that every time I drive, I worry I will crash.

There was also, however, an enormous, life-changing positive that came as a result of the accident. It seemed a fairly minor matter at the time, and it was only really made clear to me by a chance comment my mother made. As it turned out, it was that remark that started to reframe my whole life.

It was a month or so after the accident, and I had spent the weeks since worrying myself sick about my upcoming A-level results. One day my mother turned to me and said, 'Do you really think your A-level results matter after what happened? Don't you know you could not be here right now?' It was perhaps the first time that my lack of real control struck me, the realisation that this steady path through life that I had laid out for myself, and which had made so much sense to me and those around me, was actually subject to chance. Moreover, that steady path was perhaps not the most important thing after all – living, I realised, isn't really measured by grades or attainment.

I am a nervous driver to this day, but perhaps I became a little less nervous of living. I was less scared to be in disarray, on a path that wasn't calculated and curated, but wild and indirect. I became less nervous to live in chaos and discontentment. After all, if there was a chance of being sent off course anyway, what point was there in living within the narrow parameters laid out for me? What point was there in following the well-worn life paths that so many had trod before? To be honest, after that I think I often chose the path of greatest resistance, for time and time again I was drawn to environments that I didn't fit into.

Before the accident, I was looking at life through a window, strangely removed from all it had to offer. Slowly growing in a greenhouse of societal expectations, rather than in the wild garden that lay beyond. There are people who have always known they were not cut out for a conventional life. I am not one of them. I was absolutely cut out to live an extremely conventional life. I was the girl next door, and not in a mysterious, elusive way, but in a dull and particularly average way. I was an anxious person who craved stability, consistency and routine, and the product of an educational system that was very much rigged in my favour.

Yet, somehow, I haven't ended up on that path. I didn't want to create homes. I never put down roots anywhere. I have actively looked for discomfort, and then allowed that to spur me on to the next challenge. I wanted to be unpredictable, wanted my life to weave an unruly path through that wild garden, to write my own future as I went. If life was going to be unpredictable and chaotic, then so was I. It sounds counter-intuitive; this desire to be constantly slightly out of my depth; to construct a life of discomfort. It has brought with it many struggles, and a huge number of failures. Even so, I would still opt for it every single time, because it meant I felt things I never knew I could feel, and saw things I never knew I could see. Before, life had been about getting through the stages, getting from A to B by the easiest way possible, but without going through any of the turmoil that develops you as a person. I had been ticking off the levels without experiencing any of the action, and I think I knew that had to change.

It is all very well to say this, but I do owe the ability to live chaotically in huge part to my parents who, to this day, are the calm at the centre of the storm. They watched me flit from

Afghanistan to *Love Island* without a barrage of 'What if?' questions, but with a consistent concern for my well-being. They were, and remain, a constant amid continual change.

I owe it to my father, who stood at the top of the valley as I was stretchered up to the road after the accident, and who greeted me with a warm, familiar smile, looking every bit as calm and mild-mannered in the midst of the chaos as he would have done in any less fraught situation. And to my mother, who once, when she was asked by one of her friends if she worried about me when I was working abroad, replied, 'Oh not really. I don't have much of an imagination.' Whom I have always been able to call, from anywhere in the world, at any time, and who would then listen to my problems respectfully and helpfully, but almost always reminding me at the end that the most important thing was to eat and sleep. It is probably the best advice I have ever been given, even if I needed to be told, repeatedly, that problems seem far more surmountable when you are well-fed and rested.

If it was the accident that set me on that path, it took several more years for me to get to this point, to shake off fully the inconsequential things that weighed upon me. Yet even that is still only a part-truth. I am still burdened by what I feel is expected of me, both by the people I know, but also by society in general, although I am perhaps now more skilled in distinguishing these expectations and where they come from. For the most part, however, I managed to avoid the conventional path I should have followed. The only problem being that this life I chose instead has been fraught with accidents, mistakes and struggles.

Introduction

It was also on the night of the accident that I fully realised that the chaotic nature of the world makes misery at times inescapable. I only wish that, in that same moment, I had realised that this is a universal truth and not turned it inward, simply applying it to myself.

I think that something can be gleaned from living vicariously through others, and in our modern world we often simplify that idea to make it seem that we are doing so for the pleasure of watching the pain of others. That pleasure can be found in the tiniest of things, like not having a hangover while your friend groans into a plastic bag in the back of a car edging its way along the M5. I believe, however, that the idea that any joy in another's suffering is owed purely to cruelty, is wrong. In fact, I believe it is far more because we need those little insights into other people's lives in order to recognise that we are more like them, rather than less. This is a belief that is currently disappearing with the rise of the online world, which provides a platform for widely accepted ideals of perfection, and a forum for comparison.

So, often, I think that the perverse pleasure we sometimes take in someone else's suffering has far more to do with us assimilating information that makes our own self seem more bearable simply to ourselves. Our structured society and extensive online world mean that we are constantly bombarded with comparisons to our own lives, and as Theodore Roosevelt said, 'Comparison is the thief of joy.' We have reached a bizarre point where we are ever more connected, and it is ever easier to stay informed about other people's lives, and yet the knowledge we are gleaning is through two-dimensional forums where light and dark are shown in stark contrast, while the grey, shadowy areas are hidden from view.

In consequence, we are losing a huge part of the commonality we share with other people and with the world around us, a commonality born of the fact that perfection is an entirely unobtainable ideal. We are comparing our reality to another's perfect 'reality'. That is a dangerous thing to do, and makes it far more likely that we will suffer in silence, and alone, scared to represent the trials and tribulations that real life brings.

In truth, no one teaches you how to live life. Instead, you have to forge your own difficult path, often making the same mistakes others did. True, there is value in learning through pain. But there is also value in our collectively trying to pass on wisdom. To offer hope in moments of difficulty. To know that finding our own path is not all about blindly feeling around in the dark, willing ourselves forward while feeling alone.

I expect some of you are reading this because you want to learn about what it was like clearing landmines, or perhaps you want to know what appearing on *Love Island* is actually like. But maybe some of you are reading this because you feel alone. Because you feel confused and unsure.

We are, of course, different in different circumstances. We have to be to survive. That's why the first drinks with your new work colleagues are fraught with the fear that they will see the 'real you' after you have kept your head down all week. We have to adapt to fit in. You don't walk into the office with the same attitude as when you arrive at the pub. You don't confide in an acquaintance, the way you spill your guts with a friend. For many years, I believed this made me a contradictory person, and that seemed to be a bad thing, despite the fact that being varied and adaptable is an inherent part of human nature. All too frequently, I think, women have been particularly subjected to stereotyping, and to moralising assumptions that create myths about the best possible way to be a woman, which simply do not echo a nuanced reality. Perhaps this even echoes a personal reality with which we are so familiar, in which the version of ourselves that we portray to the world belies the complexities of our own selves.

Reality is so seldom what we see, and that is partly because reality is so seldom what we feel allowed to show. Often it appears the world has forgotten the funniest woman you know, who actually cries into her pillow every night. The friend who blubs all the way through even the cheesiest of chick flicks, but is consistently the calmest and most collected voice of reason. Straight-laced Jane, who loves Jägerbombs. All of these fascinating, multi-faceted gems of women, who are hidden away in the cracks because they don't fit into their neat little settings. We are narrowed and condensed into the purest form that anyone can imagine, until we are outwardly beautiful. Until we are outwardly perfect.

The fact that we are all contradictory and complex is the enemy of that perfection, and so as we are polished to look the same, we not only lose sight of the complexity of others, we lose sight of ourselves. That we can be both shy and confident. That we can be sociable and introverted. That we can be both soft and hard. This is what it means to be human, and it is what it means to grow as a person – it's what it means to be alive. Unless you are allowed to do that, it is very hard to live, and yet we are left looking around wondering where those people are – who are as flawed and confused and lost as us – because they too have had to adapt their soft, curving lines into fine straight ones to show off their best side, and fit neatly into their setting.

Yet how often is the most treasured possession the most 'perfect'? In fact, we often find perfection in imperfection: in the familiar hollow of our mattress; the scratches on the pebble brought home from the beach; the smile lines around our mother's eyes; in the stiches that hold together our favourite toy; the folds at the corners of a favourite book on the shelf; the hole in our well-worn slippers; the freckle on our best friend's cheek; in hot tea drunk from a favourite cracked mug.

I find it in my dogs, whom I love more than I ever knew I could. It is Audrey's ever so slightly wonky lower lip and crooked bottom teeth that I adore, and the white stripe behind Gus's right ear that prevents his markings being perfectly symmetrical, which I will stroke over and over again, mesmerised by these two creatures who are, to me, perfect.

It is often the absence of perfection that engages us emotionally. When we notice the missing button on an old man's shirt we wonder if there is someone at home to help him find it, and sew it back on. When we see a child with a dirty face, we wonder if there is anyone at home to wash the dirt away. There is nothing more vulnerable than an absence of perfection; nothing more human.

Yet as these ideals of perfection are the ones that we are taught to aspire to, I think often we look at doing the straightforward thing as a guarantee of outward success, and in doing so are only too willing to sacrifice our own happiness. Instead of being ourselves, we are shaped by what others think we should be.

I am a people-pleaser, there is no getting around it. I have spent much of my life trying to do the things that will win me the most praise from those around me. Yet, somehow I have found my way into places where no one expected me to be, and for me that has made all the difference between what I have done and what I was expected to do. But along the way I often felt very alone. A part of that was to do with the arenas I was in, part was to do with the way the world works, and part was to do with how I work. In truth, I look back at my younger self and I am far more impressed by her than I ever allowed myself to be at the time. I don't know now if I could do what she did. There were as many bad reasons as good for the things she did, but she was different to me now in many ways. She was impulsive and foolhardy. She felt things deeply and keenly. She was idealistic and often far more resilient than I am today.

I feel that I have a lot to learn from her, so I'm going back to find her. Most of all, I don't want her to feel alone any more, and I don't want you to feel alone, either.

Chapter 1

I Bequeath My Second Phone Charger

———

Some years later, I was twenty-three and living in Edinburgh. The accident didn't really weigh on my mind any more; I didn't have a car and I hardly ever drove. But equally the insight from the accident, as so many lessons learned when young, had been masked in the search for the easier, and quicker pleasures that distracted me from the underlying loneliness of my early twenties.

I was pretty miserable with life. As much as I had tried not to, I had in essence taken an easy path. I was working in a job that had been offered to me after I returned, with little money, to the UK from a post-university gap year. I was single. I spent most Friday nights in the company of my friends, drinking too much cheap alcohol. True, there were moments of great happiness among friends, and ridiculous antics that were both fun and funny. But overall, I do not remember it as a happy time.

Not the Type

This was before the era of Instagram quotes, but I had a faint recollection of a saying of Gandhi's: 'The best way to find yourself is to lose yourself in the service of others.' It is such a selfish way of looking at doing good, but I was twenty-three and miserable – and selfish. And I also wondered whether life could be a bit more than it was. As clichéd as that may sound, the idea began to make more sense to me. I was happiest when I could help a friend, most fulfilled when I could go the extra mile for them. Believe me, I was not a great person, not even a good one. But you can do good things for a combination of the right and wrong reasons (the same is true of bad things). People are not binary beings. There will be people you admire who also make mistakes, and people you loathe who are loving parents, and kind and loyal friends.

I was lucky in that I had travelled a bit by this stage of my life. I was, however, confused about my actual goal. I was interested in the work of war reporters and photographers such as Marie Colvin, Paul Conroy and Tim Hetherington. I had also grown up close to the headquarters of The HALO Trust, and their work in ridding former conflict zones of landmines was frequently covered in the local news. From a very young age, I had spent many hours scouring their site for information. Over and over again I was drawn back to the trust and its work.

HALO operates in current or previous conflict zones to remove explosive remnants of war (ERW). Clearing landmines is at the centre of their work. Landmines are truly the cruellest of weapons. They are explosive devices that are usually buried in the ground, and are generally victim-activated – that is, they are initiated either by standing on them, or by walking through a tripwire. In many cases they are actually designed to maim severely rather than kill people, the idea being that rather than just taking out one enemy through death, the mine takes out three – the victim and two others who have to carry the injured person. The idea of that is horrific enough, but what is truly the most horrifying thing about landmines, is the fact that they remain in the ground and function long after a conflict has ended. This means that as people displaced by war return to their homes, they run a terrible risk of falling victim to landmines, and this can continue for decades. In many areas, local knowledge builds up as accidents occur, and people begin to avoid certain routes and areas of land. This is almost equally devastating, however, as it means that many cannot carry out the activities they need to in order to survive. These marginalised communities are seldom talked about in Western mainstream media, and suffer because landmines hinder socio-economic development, trapping them in a poverty cycle that is already hard to escape, as a country rebuilds following war. In most parts of the world it is the very poorest that are affected by mines, subsistence farmers who have to choose between allowing their families to starve, or risking their lives farming land contaminated by mines.

As I have said, I often visited the HALO website. It is a good deal more modern now, but in those days it was relatively formal. I always assumed they would never accept someone like me. I considered joining the military as a route in, but I had a few moral questions about that. At that time, the HALO staff was dominated by ex-military men. I thought there was no way they would want me for anything. But I knew the value of their work. I had every faith in what they did. HALO was a place, an ideal driven by people I aspired to be like. In that, I saw a path towards becoming a person that I myself could tolerate – that I didn't loathe.

So, I decided to apply – at the time the Trust had a note on its website stating that they accepted speculative applications, but it was also known that generally they looked for people with a bit of life experience, and thus really only considered those over twenty-five. I thought, 'Maybe, I could apply and then they'll tell me what to do in the next two years to become a viable candidate.' I was invited for the interview day at the Trust's headquarters at Thornhill, less than twenty miles north of my home in Dumfries. It took place on a Friday and I spent the whole day at their office completing various tests, culminating in a panel interview with four of the senior staff, known as desk officers.

The walls of the room were covered in maps, and along the back wall was a long display shelf covered in FFE devices (FFE stands for 'free from explosives'). There were examples of mines, mortars, rockets, grenades. Guy Willoughby – one of the co-founders of HALO, which stands for 'Hazardous Area Life-support Organisation' although it is now rarely referred to as that – took me round and showed them to me, explaining how they worked, and showing me the explosive chain that made the weapon deadly.

The panel interview that followed was terrifying, I

sweated and clasped my hands under the table, all the time trying to act as though I wasn't fazed. They had a clever interview structure, where one person would ask you a question, and another member of the panel would criticise you as you answered. As far as I know, they were trying to find out whether they could wind you up. At that time, there was an assumption that it took a certain type of person to work for HALO, and that included people who could be quite extreme in their reactions, and so part of the test was designed to see if you could control yourself in tricky situations.

It was as intimidating an interview as I have ever attended. I sat at the end of the table while four of the desk officers asked me questions. Some very easy things I got wrong (it turned out I could not spell 'accommodation', although I did manage 7 multiplied by 49). The hardest questions were those that asked why I thought I was qualified to do the job, which I supposed I was in the most literal sense – but of course, part of my brain was screaming that I wasn't. I was racked with self-doubt; bizarrely, my comfort in that moment was that I usually felt like that regardless of the circumstances.

Certainly, there have been several studies that have identified that women are more likely to feel underqualified for a role than men, and thus less likely to apply for a promotion or new job, unless they are convinced they have the skills to do it. But looking at the situation objectively, I also like to give myself some benefit of the doubt here. I was a petite twenty-three-year-old in a room full of ex-military men, all experts in their trade. In the most basic sense, I was an imposter. As much as my brain was already pre-programmed to think like that, it was also reflected in the reality of the situation.

It was, of course, a stressful day, but fortunately HALO offered me a position in Cambodia as a projects officer, due to depart in just under four weeks. I was shocked, and I did momentarily question whether I was capable of the task, but I was also excited. In a strange way it felt like exactly the right thing at the right time. They sent me my contract, the medical forms, insurance papers and tax forms to register as an expatriate. The contract was unlike any other I had seen, and included items such as:

B. Overseas
1.   The Working Time Regulations apply to Great
Britain only and accordingly when working overseas
these regulations will not apply. The working day
is normally an hour before dawn to dusk, though
administrative duties may extend beyond dusk.

The week before I departed, I went to make my will. I had pretty much nothing in the bank, no possessions of any worth – perhaps the most valuable being my Babyliss roller set – but my life would be insured should I be killed or sustain a life-changing injury. I made an appointment with the same solicitor my father used. I have to be honest and admit that I barely took it seriously; 'I bequeath my second phone charger...' is hardly the stuff of a will to be read out in front of my family by a serious-faced lawyer. I think I was, if anything, pretty glib about the whole business.

Later that night I sat at home and I thought about what would happen if I did die. Not in a morbid way, in a kind of interested, abstract way, and I realised I wasn't afraid of death at all, and that, in itself, scared me. It worried me that I had lived life so carelessly that I had given myself little to live for. Despite potential, encouragement and great privilege, I had lived a life in which I saw no value. I couldn't fathom this. I had been a good student. I had left university with a first, I had travelled a bit and then joined a graduate scheme. I had started with the distinct advantages of loving parents and siblings with whom I got on well, and by then was lucky enough to have great friends – and yet I felt that a huge piece of life was somehow missing.

Once again, I was drawn back to that moment after the accident when my mother had asked, 'Do you really think your A-level results matter after what happened? Don't you know you could not be here right now?' Everything I had done so far was what, as I understood it, meant something in the world in which I had grown up. But it meant nothing to me. Beyond being slightly over-competitive, if I'm honest, I only wanted a first from university because of the way it sounded, but I didn't gain the knowledge I should have. When I was younger I loved learning, not studying but actually learning. I had a very clear idea of how much satisfaction steady improvement brings. I liked being knowledgeable. I had no idea where, along the way, I had lost that, but I certainly didn't give my degree the attention it deserved.

Other people really did give my life meaning, but I was putting all my stock in them. In myself, though, I had built nothing of which I was proud. In a way, I didn't really think I was deserving of those people around me. I certainly didn't think I was deserving of love. I am overly prone to melancholy. I am never the bubbly person in the room. I am not funny, or charismatic. I overachieved in everything bar human connection, and actually as soon as my life stopped being measured by grades or prizes, I felt lost. I couldn't find a realm in which to overachieve. I couldn't find a way to win the praise I craved, which I had enjoyed from a very young age, and which was built into every system through which I passed. Now I was to find myself in a system where satisfaction was derived only from competence, not from praise.

Cambodia

A few weeks after my interview, I boarded a plane to Sri Lanka for two weeks' training, and then went on to my posting in Cambodia. I don't think this felt as unlikely or strange as perhaps it could, or even should, have done. Maybe I had managed to prepare myself mentally. I had read through all HALO's pre-travel guidance notes for both Sri Lanka and Cambodia. I had scoured the internet for newspaper articles mentioning HALO's work in those countries. I had gone over and over any photos I could find on HALO's website, and so when I arrived, things were largely as I expected them to be. I recognised the HALO buildings, the uniforms, the personal protective equipment

(PPE). Of course, it was a very different life to the one I had been living before, but it wasn't a shock to the system in the way that might have been expected. In fact, overwhelmingly I felt relieved, and as though I had finally found my way onto the correct path.

Cambodia has a population of 16.2[1] million people. Although the poverty rate continues to fall, reaching 13.5 per cent in 2014[2], 90 per cent of those enduring poverty live in rural areas[3]. They are highly reliant on the land to survive, and many find themselves, out of economic necessity, living in close proximity to mines and other explosive remnants of war, such as unexploded mortar bombs. It is no coincidence that people living in north-western Cambodia, where there is the highest incidence of mine/ERW accidents, also experience low levels of food security, as well as restricted access to schools and hospitals, which results in a lack of access to education and poor health.

Each country where HALO has a presence has its own 'programme', and each programme is overseen by a programme manager. Three or four of these programmes are then grouped together, usually geographically, and are overseen by a desk officer, who is based in the UK. For example, the South Asia desk is made up of four programmes – Cambodia, Laos, Myanmar and Sri Lanka – each with its own programme manager based in that country. It's a similar structure to that used by the Foreign Office. Some of these

---

1 http://data.worldbank.org/country/cambodia

2 https://www.worldbank.org/en/country/cambodia/overview

3 https://www.worldbank.org/en/country/cambodia/overview

programmes are in their infancy, having been set up in the last few years, while others are well established and have run for well over a decade. Cambodia's programme had been running for roughly eighteen years when I joined.

In the first couple of weeks after I arrived in Cambodia, my desk officer was conducting a programme visit. He was (and is) very affable and intelligent, although I was reliably informed by a colleague there that he had once told a trainee that if the latter pointed to a map with his finger again, he, the desk officer, would cut it off. You never point at a map with your finger because, even with tiny fingers like my own, doing so does not provide you with pinpoint accuracy. You should use a pointer stick, if available – there was one in every HALO office I ever visited (I also knew someone who carried a retractable pointer stick wherever he went). Failing that, you would use the next most suitable pointed item you had to hand – a sharpened pencil, for instance.

As part of his visit, the desk officer often spends a week in the field, travelling around HALO's area of operations with the programme manager, and this time, I am asked to accompany them so that the trip can double as my familiarisation with the country programme. Among visits to current minefield tasks (i.e. tasks where HALO has clearance teams working), the desk officer is also there to review the minefields they have put on the clearance plan for next year. At each site, we climb out of the Land Rovers and the programme manager unfurls a large map. We all crowd around as he points at it (with an appropriate implement) and briefs us on why this site in particular should be a priority for clearance, for instance by indicating the presence of local landowners, or where the map shows a school or medical centre.

I notice that the desk officer's pointer of choice is frequently a sharp stem or blade of dried grass picked from the side of the road. The first time he asks me to point something out on a map, I picked my blade of grass hoping that he would be impressed that I didn't point with my finger. Unfortunately, despite using the correct implement, I identified completely the wrong location on the map, but at least I retained my full complement of digits. The desk officer returned to the UK after a further few days spent in the HALO Cambodia HQ in Siem Reap, and I have never pointed at a map with my finger again (and am known to fuss about this even now on the very few occasions in my current life when a paper map is required).

My life transformed incredibly quickly in the weeks that followed. I was based in the country headquarters in Siem Reap, and spent time travelling between the three regional bases in Anlong Veaeng, Banteay Meanchey and Battambang. I had been hired as a response to a requirement for more extensive data collection to measure the impact of mine clearance. The charity sector is a competitive one, and organisations consistently have to apply for grants, as well as appealing to the public for their financial support. To do that successfully, charities need to be able to show the value of the work they are doing. I joined the programme when it had 800 national staff in Cambodia, with myself and my boss, the programme manager, as international staff. HALO ran an extremely lean expatriate structure, for two reasons.

Firstly, it is a much more economical way of running an organisation like HALO, because international flights and staff are expensive. Secondly, there is often no need for international staff – many of the country programmes I worked on had been running for a very long time, and the institutional knowledge, skill and experience of the senior local staff were exceptional.

The projects officer role was unique in a way, since it did require the ability to speak English because of the complex donor reports, and that's why HALO was looking for an international member of staff to handle them. These donor reports were mainly for the large grants received through the foreign-aid budgets of various countries, including the UK and the USA. I also wrote reports for the larger grants provided by family foundations, which tended to be less focused on data analysis and statistics, and more on case studies. There was also a huge amount that needed to be done in terms of developing the structures and systems for data collection and analysis, and this formed a large section of the job specification that had been written by the programme manager for my arrival, since it was a new role for the Cambodia programme. In fact, that's why I was sent to Sri Lanka to train, because the HALO programme there was the only one that had had a projects officer for a few months.

I had my notes from Sri Lanka, but many things were different in Cambodia – the same role in HALO can vary widely between countries because of the diverse challenges. Cambodia was one of HALO's largest, but also second-oldest programme. Because of that, I was able to learn a lot, but equally it is hard to drop into such a well-established programme, where everyone knows exactly what they are doing, with the remit for a brand-new position. There were best practices to be established; the role, and its purpose, were still being carved out. This felt like a lot of pressure, almost as if I had to justify my existence. Equally, I enjoyed the fact that there wasn't someone there already handing over the role to me. The work was more challenging, and definitely more time-consuming, but I did like the freedom I had to research and plan out how to do things. I just felt the need for guidance and support while I was doing it, to ensure that what I was doing was useful, and also to be able to justify its use to teams who had been working in mine clearance for almost two decades.

I was, I think, initially influenced by some of the established ways in which HALO had historically worked, and I worried a lot about implementing new practices, or adding to the workload of staff without being able to justify why. I was also very accepting of the 'It's always been done this way' attitude. But three months into my time there, my first programme manager departed, and the man who came to replace him was of the type who questions everything, asking how it could be made more efficient. He was very quick to see areas that could be improved, and could identify the gaps in seemingly unquestionable processes with ease. I was very fortunate to learn from him. He was a very fair boss, but I can't deny that I was terrified of him at first – he was extremely intelligent, and would often have already joined all the dots together in a conversation, and so be about ten steps ahead of me when we spoke. I had a lot of conversations with him during which I nodded along with a knowing look on my face, and then rushed back to my desk afterwards to try to figure out exactly what I was meant to do. However, his oversight of the programme moved things along significantly for my role. He helped find the correct solutions, software and hardware, to some of the struggles we faced when it came to remote management. For example, we began trialling conducting pre- and post-clearance surveys using forms that were filled out on tablets, rather than on paper. This meant that the data was returned to us at HQ every night once the tablets were synced, rather than in a pile of paper delivered at the end of each month when the teams returned from the field.

Many of the socio-economic studies that I worked on for HALO in Cambodia were designed to measure whether families had been raised above the poverty line after the mines had been cleared. It seemed to be such an exact science when I first learnt about it. The poverty line was measured annually, and when we would first interview families we would ask how much money they lived on per family member per day. When we interviewed families at six and twelve months after clearance, it was evident that families that had started out with more assets or a higher level of income found it easiest to move above the poverty line. This absolutely stands to reason; it is a smaller jump for them to move above the line and they have a greater ability to do so. It took far longer for those who were devastatingly impoverished to move above the line. Similarly, it took longer for families that had a member who suffered physical or mental illness, partly due to there being fewer working members of the family, and partly because of medical costs. We would often ask them what obstacles they faced in using their land now that it was free from landmines, and these would frequently relate to lack of equipment like tractors. It was also often related to their lack of transport to take their produce to market. Instead, local traders would come to them, but this invariably meant that they were offered the lowest price for their crops.

Bizarrely, many of the reporting procedures required to ensure the conditions for government grants were met, do not serve the extremely vulnerable and marginalised. Helping the poorest people in the most difficult circumstances does not show immediate gains. One of the measures that is often used to oversee the value of the money that has been invested in humanitarian projects, is improvements in beneficiaries' socio-economic status. However, it can take months, and often, for the most vulnerable, years before these accumulate enough to be quantifiable in terms of a survey (although often the benefits have already been felt by the family in a slow and steady gain). Grants, however, tend to require assessment within at least twelve months, and so reports often don't reflect these small, incremental gains made over time. In that sense, it is those who are just below the poverty line that end up looking the most favourable, since helping them will make the project appear to have been been more effective. To HALO's endless credit, they argued and explained this point time and time again, and they continued, and continue, to help the poorest and most vulnerable.

Yet it is clear that often reporting in this way incentivises helping those in relatively more prosperous circumstances. That type of reporting structure has predominantly come from business practice in the West, which measures efficiency and return as the primary goals. This is interesting in itself, for it calls into question how often the poor are truly prioritised within societies that look to encourage wealth above all else. How does this play out in terms of fairness and equality? Essentially, it doesn't. In fact, in many ways equality is seen almost as the antithesis of progress, because it is a balancing-out effect, rather than a gains effect. When talking about 'markets' or even 'poverty lines', there is often a sense of abstraction about what this actually means for people. This is not to say that numbers and measures aren't helpful, but it is important to remember the context of these figures, how they have been calculated, and the origins of such calculations – for example, whether that particular type of measurement is rooted in capitalism. Figures can be misunderstood or misused, sometimes in order to conceal a reality in which a number can be used to indicate an improvement that may only be significant for an already advantaged minority, so perpetuating existing inequalities.

Cambodia marked the first time that I had truly lived somewhere different. I had travelled during my gap year, but only now did I realise that I been in the travelling bubble, flitting from place to place as a spectator, someone of little to no consequence to those who actually lived in the places I visited, except perhaps when I bought the odd knick-knack in a gift shop. Now I suddenly felt overwhelming pressure to adapt to my environment, but at the same time to recognise and acknowledge that I did not belong. I did not belong because of my privileged background, and this inequality became yet more evident in the months that passed. I was too lucky, my life too fortunate, and there was no way to reconcile that with what I saw around me. This devastated me and educated me in equal measure. I felt complicit in that inequality, because I have benefited, and continue to benefit, from living in a developed country.

It was also my first taste of watching from a distance life play out in another place without me: family occasions from which I was absent; friends meeting new friends, and my no longer being a part of the gang. Each time I went to check Facebook I would suffer a horrible feeling of fear, and then an icy trickle down my spine as I watched best friends make new best friends, and exes meet new girlfriends. Eventually I stopped checking Facebook, and I wasn't that into WhatsApp messaging either. Otherwise, I felt I would be living an almost half life, caught up in the fact that my life might have followed either of two very different trajectories.

I am often asked why I don't have a Scots accent. Neither of my parents is originally Scottish, although I do remember my dad cheerfully attesting that we are descendants of the Vikings, so perhaps we can claim more Scottish heritage than I give us credit for. My parents moved to Scotland before my older sister was born. I was born there in 1989, and have always felt Scottish. It is a place that does instil national pride from the very start. But truthfully, my love of the country comes from more than living north of Hadrian's Wall. Yes, I loved the sense of community there, but I also loved the countryside. My childhood was spent happily outdoors, often barefoot. I love Scotland, and always will. To this day if you ask me what 'home' is like, I automatically assume you are talking about Scotland.

I never had a strong Scots accent, but I did have a lilt and I loved it. At university, I really enjoyed the moments when people noticed it. I suspect that I probably thought it made me more interesting, and I didn't feel particularly interesting otherwise. When I went to work abroad, however, I found that a Scots accent is not the easiest for a translator to understand. In Cambodia I worked closely with a translator who became a great friend, and we continue to email each other to this day. Her spoken English was excellent, and I think that, working alongside her, my accent softened, and I was careful to be understood.

The space that I had occupied had started to evaporate, mainly because it never really existed in the first place. It was the space society had created for me, in which I had felt obliged to place myself. We only live within these spaces because we are taught that they have a real existence, that they are real places. They aren't. They are a figment of our socio-political imaginations. But without my own space, I couldn't find another way to define myself, to fit in, to belong. There wasn't another space. In Shaw's *Pygmalion*, following elocution lessons Eliza says to her teacher, 'You told me, you know, that when a child is brought to a foreign country, it picks up the language in a few weeks, and forgets its own. Well, I am a child in your country. I have forgotten my own language, and can speak nothing but yours.' For her it became impossible to go back into the world from which she came.

In my case, it wasn't that I learnt Khmer, the official language of Cambodia. I picked up a few useful words and phrases here and there; I could greet people and I could count, but I was never proficient in it. I didn't adopt the language of a new country. I was still ostensibly from the UK, but the way I spoke its language changed. Some might have said that I became more well-spoken, that I had acquired a greater mastery of English, but slowly the Scottish lilt disappeared. It felt as though this marked the distance that was opening up between me and the life I had known before. I felt malleable, shapeable, adaptable – all useful qualities when you are travelling around working.

I often think about the translator that I worked with during that time. She was a year younger than I, and together we travelled along the heavily mined border with Thailand, collecting case studies of families who had lost loved ones, or whose members had themselves been injured. We met young children who had lost legs, families struggling to survive after the father had been killed working their land, others with starving children because their land was contaminated with mines. That is a terrible choice to have to make, whether to risk your life to feed your family, when the consequences might lead to your family starving anyway. And that's what kept striking me, time and again: what terrible, heart-wrenching choices people were having to make. Do I send my children to school, when I know the only way to get there is to walk through a minefield? There's a chance that one or more will tread on a mine and die, but if they aren't educated there is also every chance they will be trapped in the poverty cycle and not have much of a life anyway. Horrific choices. People very rarely end up with a bad lot in life because of bad choices they have made. They are far more likely to make bad choices because of their bad lot in life. What is even worse than that, however, is people being trapped in a situation in which they cannot make a good choice. To me, it was extraordinary that people could be living with such a harsh reality, and yet their plight should be known so little outside their own country.

My role in Cambodia was predominantly administrative. Much of it involved working with the Data and GIS team in the main office in Siem Reap. GIS refers to 'geographic information systems', and with it we produced various maps with different overlays, allowing us to see the correlation between two different data sets – for example, minefields and poverty level per administrative district. A lot of the data that was already being collected was centred on operations, but there was now a demand for further information that showed the impact of such work, rather than just relying on the assumption that there would be benefits. It stands to reason that mine clearance is a good thing, not only because every landmine removed represents a potential life or limb saved, but also in terms of access to agricultural land for crops, as well as to areas on which to build schools, or to provide safe routes to medical facilities. Understandably, however, donors were looking to measure what this impact was, and this was important for HALO too – it helped us identify areas where there was the most pressing need for clearance, as well as the areas where we could make the greatest difference. Although collecting such information was something HALO did as a matter of course, through extensive localised knowledge, having the data that was systematically collected to back this up undoubtedly helped strengthen future planning. The move to this kind of data for reports was, however, in part due to a wider change in the charity sector, where the requirements of donors now included their being shown the measurable impact of the work that they were funding, as well as a shift towards a competitive tendering process for bigger government grants. This meant that organisations had to bid for grants, requiring you to quantify not only the actual work that could be done with a given sum of money, but also the impact of that work.

It is very straightforward to measure and record the progress of operational mine clearance: you can easily count the number of mines destroyed, the area of land cleared, and the number of minefields completed. However, what does that actually translate to in terms of the impact for the communities that the clearance is serving? How many landowners had their land restored, and how did they plan to use it? What was the financial value of the crops grown on cleared land? How did this correspond to raising families above the poverty line? How many schools were built on cleared land, and how many children now had access to primary education as a result? My job was to collect and collate such information, and in order to do so I also spent a fair amount of time in the field, usually taking a trip to one of HALO's three locations during each working cycle.

A working cycle usually refers to a twenty-one-day work period. During this time, deminers work every day, and between these cycles they take six or seven days' leave, which is referred to as 'standdown'. This works well because most deminers have to stay in remote camps close to the minefields they are clearing. Returning home every weekend would mean that they would lose much of their time off to travel. In addition, from a logistics perspective, using these cycles meant that all the necessary equipment only had to be transported to a site once.

The deminers' working day was broken down into half-hour shifts, separated by ten-minute breaks. During the thirty-minute shifts, deminers wear their full PPE including their visors, which are relatively heavy and uncomfortable. The ten-minute breaks between the shifts give them a chance to remove their visors, have a drink of water and a break. During the hot season in Cambodia, particularly in April and May, temperatures soar and the heat is oppressive. The concentration required during clearance is very high. However, deminers are also carrying out an activity that is largely repetitive. Breaking the working day up like this meant that the teams were productive and maintained a high degree of accuracy.

HALO was working across an area of operations that

covered four provinces: Otdar Meanchey, Banteay Meanchey, Battambang and Pailin, with the main administrative office located in Siem Reap. One of the locations in which I spent a lot of time was our remote office in Otdar Meanchey, which was based in the town of Anlong Veaeng. We had a particular project running there, where we had partnered with an agricultural NGO to ensure that impoverished landowners also received support in returning their agricultural land to use following clearance of mines, and I collected several case studies to see whether the partnership had worked successfully.

The building was located next to a small lake, and frequently flooded during the rainy season. There was another problem that came with the rainy season, and that was rats. They were unlike any other rats I have ever seen, nearer in size to a small cat than a rat. In fact, the location manager did at one point get a cat to try to keep the rats away, but they were so large and intimidating that they chased the cat away and it was never seen again.

At night, the rats would run along the beams above the network of bedrooms. You would hear them scuttling along, and if you looked up, you would see their furry silhouettes, sometimes pausing to glance down, and then scuttling on to the next bedroom. They also had a disgusting habit of getting hold of any clothes they could find, and they were partial to gnawing through the armpits of dirty T-shirts, or the crotch of dirty trousers. Sometimes they'd pull a T-shirt partway through gaps between the floorboards, and in the morning when you went to pick it up, you would find that it had become a crop top.

Not the Type

Although all the rooms were separated by wooden walls, they didn't have ceilings and the walls only went as high as the beams, with the inverted V of the roof above. So the rats could run along the wooden beams between the rooms. One night there was a particularly persistent rat, scuttling around my room. It had grown in confidence, and was running down into the room and trying to get into my bag. I kept shooing it away, and it would run up the wall, along the wooden beams, and into the bedroom of the location manager opposite. I would then hear him shooing the same rat out of his room, and it would come running back over to mine. In the end I found it very comical, although not particularly conducive to a good night's sleep.

To be honest, things like that don't really bother me much. I quite liked the story of the rats; I enjoyed telling it to people at home, and watching their shocked reaction. I'm not particularly squeamish, and I also wanted to experience the 'rough and ready' side of things. In Cambodia, I wasn't clearing mines myself during the day. I was going out and collecting information and compiling and assessing data to explain why mine clearance was, and is, so important. My life was rough and ready in a way, but very much manageably so, and although those days in the field were long, dusty and hot, they were also interesting and there was a sense of adventure to them. We would get to drive to cleared land and look at the crops that had grown, stopping by on the way to meet the landowner, and asking if he would mind if we took a picture of him with his newly grown cassava plants.

I Bequeath My Second Phone Charger

Yet I heard so many terrible stories during the eighteen months I spent in Cambodia. I remember in particular visiting one accident site, where a woman and her husband had been out with their two young children, collecting wood to build their house before the rainy season began. They had been piling timber into their buffalo cart and the mother was worried that the cart would be too heavy for the animal if they all sat on it, and so she followed it on foot, walking behind her young family. Minutes from their home the cart ran over an anti-tank mine, killing her husband, her son and her daughter before her eyes. The team that went to help clear the site found the limbs of her husband and children in the trees surrounding the mine crater.

On another occasion, a man told me of the evening he went out to collect wood in one of the forested areas that run along the border. On his way back home, he stepped on an anti-personnel mine, which caused a traumatic amputation of his lower left leg. It is called a traumatic amputation for a reason. The injuries from a landmine are not neat. They are horrendous ragged-edged wounds, filled with shards of bone and dirt fired straight up into the burnt, blackened skin. They are a mangled mess of red, black and white where there once was a functioning limb. They result in agonising pain and shock no matter to whom they happen, trained soldier or young child. As I have said, landmines are actually intended to maim their victims, rather than kill them. Now imagine that happening to a father farming his land to grow food for his family, to a mother carrying her baby to the nearby health centre, to a child walking to school. As long as landmines remain in the ground, this is the risk ordinary people face, these are the accidents that are waiting to happen.

In this instance, the victim was miles from home, all alone, and it was raining. No one knew where he was, leaving him with no choice but to try to make it back to where he lived. He managed to crawl a couple of miles, until he reached a small stream he had crossed on his way into the forest. Because of the rain, it was now a rushing river and there was no way he could get across it, so he used his thin shirt as a tourniquet, and dragged himself under a tree to wait out the night. He was there alone, in shock, losing blood, in the rain and the cold. Eventually, the next morning, the rain stopped and he crawled home. There wasn't a medical centre near where he lived, so his family loaded him on to a cart and took him on a journey of several hours to a medical centre where he could be operated on. He told me this whole story with a smile on his face, and this makes me uncomfortable when I think about it now. Smiling or laughing is frequently a sign of awkwardness; it is also often an indicator that someone is trying to tell an uncomfortable truth to another person who, for whatever reason, cannot identify with what is being said. The truth is, this situation was extremely uncomfortable. The injured man was telling me of an experience that simply could never have happened to me, and no matter how much I wanted to understand, I was never going to.

There is, too, another disjoint in this: a shameful irony so deeply entrenched that perhaps we don't even recognise it as an irony. It was I who was going to tell that story. I would sit at my desk and write it up, perhaps adding a photograph of the man with his family, perhaps one with his prosthetic leg, and that write-up would be put into donor reports to explain to donors that they needed to keep funding mine clearance, or would perhaps appear on the website to encourage more private donations from the public.

When you are writing up a case study, you are always trying, as much as possible, to make it true to the subject's voice, but inevitably it will be affected by your own. By the time an account has been translated to you, and you have written it up in a way that fits the style of report you are trying to write, it is marked by your hand. I tried to write things as factually as possible, but from the very minute you start to use words to link sentences together, or to explain the impact of events on someone else's life, your voice is in there. Often, especially for items that will be used in public-facing communications such as a website, you are looking to balance emotion with the facts, in a way that will incentivise people to understand the gravity of what is happening, and thus donate. So your account will differ from how it was relayed to you by the person whose story it is, and however well intended, those added layers of emotion are what you have inferred from your understanding of the facts.

I often think about this now, and there are many dangerous narratives that we unwittingly string together as privileged people whose voices are heard. So many of the people I met in Cambodia, who had very little in the way of possessions, seemed happier than many I knew back home who ostensibly had everything they could ever have hoped for. I now feel very uncomfortable reflecting upon how I viewed this at that time, particularly my remarking upon how many people I saw in Cambodia who seemed so happy, despite having so little. I began to realise that this ill-informed view was actually propagating a dangerous narrative. People survive – it is what we are designed to do. We survive with what we have. People can still fall in love, forge friendships, find joy in nature, but we observers should not mistake the momentary joys of living for someone being perpetually happy. In particular, we should not assume that it is their lack of material possessions, and especially not their lack of access to modern healthcare, education, and even food and water, that enables them to live 'such a carefree life'. This is so clear to me now that I am ashamed to have ever felt differently about it. How many of us have smiled through the bad circumstances? Have used humour to mask pain? We are designed for self-preservation. That people survive with so little deserves our respect; many of us will never have to find out whether we are resilient enough to do the same. But it is not for us to say that these people are happier than we are because they don't have to deal with the trappings of social media, or similar pressures that we do.

It's actually really grim that we see their suffering as some form of enlightenment. It is not. It only exposes the way in which we seek to justify the imbalanced structures that form the backbone of our social, political and economic systems. A major part of why this myth continues to be perpetuated is because all too often people's stories are not told by themselves, but by the person of privilege or power, and this means we end up with an extremely one-sided view of the world. It was not for me to tell these stories to my friends at home, and yet I did. But perhaps that was part of the reason why I found the experience so jarring.

There was something extremely uncomfortable in this that was becoming ever clearer to me, and yet the right way to move forward was becoming more confusing. The reason why mine clearance appealed to me, and why I consider it to be so absolutely necessary, is because it's not like giving someone a food parcel, which is eaten and then it's gone. It is a tangible way to provide them with the land they need to be able to grow food for their families or to sell, or access routes to water sources, schools and medical centres. The impacts of clearance are felt first by those who have been denied access to that land, but the benefits are sustained and ongoing, because once mines are cleared, they are gone for ever. There is an empowering quality to it, for it removes an obstacle that presents a threat both to lives and livelihoods, and in doing so, aims to facilitate a pathway to people rebuilding their own lives.

Even so, mine clearance only removes one of many obstacles that face conflict-affected, marginalised, poverty-stricken communities, and so whilst I was aware of actively trying to do something tangible to improve things, at exactly the same moment I was alarmed at how little I had known about these difficulties before, because I myself was unaffected by them. Perhaps more alarmingly, working in Cambodia was my first proper encounter with how discomforting that is to confront, as well as with the complexities of deciding how best to play a part in changing things.

This was why I had an increasing desire to work on the operational side, and I became quite consumed by that. It means working within the actual process of mine clearance, so, for example, you could be a location manager, whose job is to oversee all clearance on sites within a particular area. To do so, you need to have the appropriate explosive ordnance disposal qualifications to ensure the correct methods are deployed at each site, and that operations are being conducted safely. You also need the requisite skills in logistics, planning, store management and a whole host of other abilities required to keep the process running safely and efficiently. In order to qualify to work on these practical elements of the process, you have to go through HALO's training course and so I began to ask if I could do that. To be honest, I don't think the organisation ever intended for me to go through that training. I wasn't really an obvious candidate, but by the end of 2014, there were new recruits being taken on to work in operations, including a woman, Susanna, who later became a friend. There had also been, in that year, another male projects officer (the position I had) who had joined the operations training course.

I became intent on doing it. It made me believe that I would be doing something more tangible, I would be being more constructive and actually adding some action to what I was learning about, rather than merely peering into other people's lives. I was confused about how much impact I was making, and found my position of advantage uncomfortable partly because I was often talking about and justifying the benefits of a process of which I didn't have first-hand experience.

I Bequeath My Second Phone Charger

The projects officer role also seemed relatively cushy, and I felt that having my boots on the ground would mean more. I continued to express my interest in the operations course at every opportunity, very possibly to the frustration and annoyance of my superiors, but by the end of 2014, I was given the opportunity to travel to Nagorno-Karabakh in the coming January, to begin my operations training.

Chapter 2

The Alfresco Wee

I had heard very little about Nagorno-Karabakh before I went to work there. This landlocked area in the South Caucasus lies geographically within the borders of Azerbaijan, but is mainly inhabited by Armenians. This was no accident. The oblast – a Russian word for an administrative division – was originally formed in the early 1920s as an instrument of the Stalinist divide-and-conquer policy in the region, itself a part of the Soviet Union's long-term agenda in Turkey. In 1988, clashes broke out between Armenia and Azerbaijan over which had official control over the area, conflict that essentially stemmed from the two countries' opposing views over whether territory or national identity was more important in determining ownership of an area.

In 1991, both Armenia and Azerbaijan became independent from the Soviet Union, and the violence over Nagorno-Karabakh escalated. This conflict lasted until May

1994, and resulted in thousands of casualties and hundreds of thousands of refugees. A ceasefire agreement was struck and peace talks began, led by the OSCE Minsk Group,[4] which are fascinating for many reasons, not least because whilst Armenia and Azerbaijan are represented, Nagorno-Karabakh is not. Thus far, they have provided no resolution and the ceasefire has also proved difficult to maintain, with multiple violations by both sides. As recently as April 2016, numerous news outlets covered a re-eruption of violence along the frontline, resulting in the deaths of thirty people.

The historic Soviet oblast boundary no longer stands as the accepted border, because during the war the Armenian Karabakhis managed to take control of the shortest route between Nagorno-Karabakh and Armenia; an area known as the Lachin corridor. It is along this route that I was first driven to the capital, Stepanakert, after landing in Yerevan in January 2015.

Nagorno-Karabakh is also a place of staggering beauty, impressively mountainous and forested. I arrived in the depths of winter, when a cold mist hung over the grey buildings of the capital Stepanakert giving it a seemingly bleak air, but this contrasted with the warmest of welcomes. The people are renowned for their hospitality, unendingly generous with their food: jars of pickles, fresh bread, boiled eggs, soft white cheese, ginger buns, shashlik with potatoes cooked on a spit. On every pavement corner is a group of men huddled together, talking and smoking slimline cigarettes, invariably

---

[4] Established in the 1970s, the Organisation for Security and Cooperation in Europe is the largest inter-state body concerned with security in the world. Participating countries include the UK, the USA, Russia and all major European nations, as well as Armenia and Azerbaijan.

dressed in black leather jackets. In the evenings they gather in bars, toasting war heroes over carafes of mulberry vodka.

As you drive north towards the hot springs and Dadivank monastery, the roads are regularly and touchingly marked by war memorials: disused tanks, piles of bullet-ridden helmets intermingled with flowers, fresh water springs built in remembrance. It is impossible to adequately capture in photographs the sorrow in the empty villages as you pass through them. Bullet holes riddle the walls of deserted buildings. Homesteads that became battlegrounds; one scarred by a rush of bullet holes diagonally across a stone wall, meeting the corner of a metal bedframe on the other side. There are fields criss-crossed with trenches, mountainsides marked by small shelters, almost always with a grave listing the names who died there.

The schools display photographs of their pupils who fought and died. Young men and women who did not live beyond their teens, a stark reminder of the reality of a war of which few people in the West have ever heard. Whilst the human cost of the conflict is overwhelmingly tragic, there are few things more humbling than witnessing a love of such epic proportions; a kinhood forged in the kiln of the uneasy meeting point of the Russian, Persian and Ottoman Empires. The paradigmatic example of the immeasurable power of conflict to unite people; that which intends to divide forming the closest bonds of all.

There is no other place quite like it; a demi-paradise set against a backdrop of mortar fire as the front-line murmurs on. The region is small enough that at some of the locations where we worked, you could actually hear the daily rumble of firing at the frontline. Although this was largely accepted as being for display purposes, in April 2016 the clashes escalated and dozens of people were killed, reportedly including civilians on both sides, among them a twelve-year-old boy.

Nagorno-Karabakh: demining

My alarm would go off at 3:50am, and I'd drag myself out of bed and get ready for the long day ahead. I used to put on two pairs of thermal leggings, two pairs of thermal socks – thin ones that are warm but will fit inside my boots – a pair of black fleece-lined work trousers, a thermal vest and two thermal under layers, a base layer fleece, a thick over fleece, and finally a down jacket. I would check the pocket of my trousers to make sure I had my Leatherman (a folding pocket knife with several other tools besides blades) and a few mini chocolate bars. I'd tie my hair back and put on my woolly hat, and head with my fellow trainee down the stairs into the cold. Every morning, a grey mist would hang over Stepanakert and it was too dark to see much apart from a thin layer of frost over the Nivas (tiny Soviet 4x4s) parked on either side of the street.

Around twelve of us, eleven burly men and me, would climb into a little battered minibus and begin to drive north, the music alternating between extreme Euro pop, and recognisable British tracks. Despite how loud it was, I would occasionally doze off and slip off my seat much to the amusement of the rest of the bus. At the base of a mountain we would stop and meet the team members who are living on-site because they wouldn't be able to travel there daily – not everyone lives in the capital Stepanakert. After we get out and regroup into our sections the minibus heads off, back to Stepanakert, and we climb into the collection of Land Rovers and Land Cruisers parked at the base of the mountain. They are old and battered, little of the internal upholstery remains but they still run, mainly due to the work of extremely resourceful mechanics who maintain them. They are already crammed to the brim with detector boxes and major trauma medic kits but somehow we all pile in around them with our tool bags and body armour.

The road up to the minefield bends and weaves around the edge of the lower Caucasus mountains. Even though it's icy, the driver takes it at pace knowing we can't afford to get stuck as we may not get started again. It's just passing 6am as we near the top, and the road turns into a mud track just before the parking area that has been prepared in front of the minefield where the teams will deploy. The last vehicle has the hardest task, the earlier arrivals have melted the snow and the mud has become sticky. It roars to the top, at the last second sliding through the thick mud into place beside the others. The vehicles are always parked in the direction of departure so that they are ready for a casualty evacuation should an accident occur.

I head with my section to our allotted portion of a massive minefield that spans the mountaintop. It is clear why it would be useful tactically, but now it is an area where the locals forage, and they need to be able to do so safely. Together we prepare a fire, unload the vehicle and set up the medical point sheltered from snow by a blue tarpaulin. The stretcher is laid out ready to be used if necessary, and the major trauma kit placed next to it. Once the fire is going, strong coffee is made quickly, it is two centimetres in a cup, thick, grainy and delicious, very similar to Turkish coffee but you absolutely NEVER say that. Nearly everyone smokes, vogue slimline cigarettes are uncommonly popular, and the men seem to suck them down in two drags. Each unpacks a detector and grabs their tool bag and we all head to the start of our lanes to carry on clearance from the day before.

Somehow, I've ended up with a lane on a 45-degree angle which exactly coincides with where, not all that long ago, someone must have emptied a full magazine firing at their enemy, so the ground is laced with bullet casings. When you are looking for mines the first step is to run the detector over the ground in front of you. Each signal needs to be marked and carefully excavated. So, every bullet casing is throwing up a signal, which I then isolate and carefully excavate towards to find out if it is a mine. The ground is frozen solid and even with two pairs of gloves on my fingers feel cold to the bone, the metal tools start to stick to the gloves as they freeze in your hands. As you breathe it turns to ice on the inside of the visor, and a light dusting of snow continues to fall. I know I cannot be lulled into a false sense of security. Not every signal is necessarily a bullet casing. Every excavation must be as precise as the last.

All the deminers are male, many fought in the conflict

and are ready to serve again should the need arise. The chief course instructor has a scar that runs down the side of his face where he was shot, the bullet narrowly missing his eye.

The society is conservative and it's rare to see women in the few bars and restaurants in Stepanakert. When I arrived in Nagorno-Karabakh with my male colleague to complete operations training, we couldn't find our pick-up driver – it turned out he was there all along but he didn't come over because he was expecting two men. I do feel an immense responsibility to prove myself. It's now February 2015. I was in Cambodia from July 2013 to December 2014, and out of those eighteen months, I spent at least a year hoping to be selected for this course, and I try to keep that in my mind whenever it gets tough. After a few days your back stops aching, it stops feeling strange to be cold and tired – actually it's quite enjoyable. Every time I go to carry my bag someone will try and take it from me, but I politely decline with a 'spasiba' – Russian for thank you. Definitely an element of this need to prove myself is in my head, but I know how easy it would be for my gender and diminutive stature to be an excuse for me to fail, in their eyes and my own.

Actually, my main problem quickly becomes working out how to go for a pee! It sounds odd, but you can't be out from 4 a.m. to 4 p.m., drink copious amounts of coffee, and drink enough water to keep you going when you are physically working, without at some point needing the loo. In Karabakh, the working schedule is slightly different from that in Cambodia. We do fifty-minute shifts with five-minute breaks (funnily enough, the break literally translates as 'smoking break' due to the prevalence of cigarette smoking). Five minutes is enough for the guys to nip behind a bush and have a quick pee if they need to. But I would have to find somewhere with enough coverage to be private (remembering this is an incredibly conservative culture), but that is also within the safe ground that is already cleared. The options are extremely limited. Any obvious locations are too far to walk there and back in five minutes.

For the first couple of days, I cross my legs and hold it. My body is already tense from the cold weather, and I'm so cold I almost feel like any wee I might have is frozen anyway, but I can't keep that up. I have a headache by the end of both days, and I know I should be drinking more water. I've known staff in other places complaining of UTIs because they haven't been drinking enough water. This is rare now as more women have been employed, SOPs (standard operating procedures) regarding latrines have been improved. Usually, you dig a hole as soon as you start work at a minefield (in a cleared area of course), and put up blue tarpaulins to ensure there is adequate cover for privacy. However, this isn't really a thing in Karabakh. I'm only the second woman they have ever had working on the minefield, and there's no real need for them to dig a latrine at every site. There's one at the Control Point (about fifteen minutes' walk back from the minefield), but I can't spend half an hour walking there and back as I would miss nearly a full working session.

I think about the best way to approach the issue. As much as it is not worth risking my health or any lack of concentration through dehydration, equally I am wary of making it an issue. It would set me apart from the group, and I know it would make many of the male staff there feel uncomfortable. I am definitely in a man's domain here. I know it seems that perhaps I should have just barrelled in and said something, that perhaps they should feel uncomfortable, that perhaps that was progress, but I wasn't convinced that would get me anywhere. I do think this happened without ill-intentions. When a system has built up with only men within it, there are oversights when it comes to providing for women's needs. That is worth remembering in a wider context, so much of society has been built with men as the focus. Challenging that is often seen as controversial, but these oversights are important.

With the help of my fellow (male) trainee who spoke Russian, I broached the subject with the team leader at the start of one working day. He listened quietly, and asked me to give him some time to sort it. After the first work session he came up and showed me to a sheltered spot in a corner of the cleared section of the minefield, about 50 metres from where I was working. It was well hidden, and easy for me to get to, and made an enormous difference to my subsequent experience working in the field. There was no fuss, it was as small a deal as it could possibly have been, and yet it made an enormous difference to me.

It may sound like I am making a very big deal out of an alfresco wee, but actually I had learnt a lot about how important these issues can be, mainly from other NGOs more focused on the provision of WASH facilities, which I had encountered in Sri Lanka when I was training, and others in Cambodia.

It really isn't well-known enough how crucial private WASH facilities are in the protection of women and children from violence, particularly in refugee camps, and also notably in slums. I'm not suggesting my situation was comparable, but it was an eye-opener to how these seemingly small things can be quite easily overlooked, and in more unstable and insecure situations, that can have far greater consequences.

It's not just about safety (although that must remain paramount), it is also about respect. It's degrading for someone to have to feel embarrassed because the correct provisions haven't been made to fulfil their basic needs. It sends a message that they are considered less relevant than the default person they 'expect' to be doing that job. Sometimes these things did feel personal. In most places where I worked for HALO, where there were female employees, there was never any appropriately fitting uniform. It was all just small male sizes, which were ill-fitting. When working in Georgia, I lived in an adapted container, because the house being used as the staff base was all-male. I was there in the summer and the temperatures rose to the 30s daily, and the container was unbearably hot by the time I was able to go to bed in the evening.

Certainly, issues were dealt with well in Karabakh, but there were other times over the years when the systems that had been built upon typically masculine tenets of strength, seemed too delicate to deal with being challenged. In fact, I found I had to be incredibly careful in my voicing of issues, and often focus on their need for any criticism to be levelled in a particular way, rather than actually focus on the problem.

In my experience, there were some staff that reacted incredibly badly when issues were raised, or perhaps belittled the nature of them. I could see where this attitude stemmed from. When you are working in life-and-death situations, it is hard to see the importance of clothing and loos. Or you might be inclined to think, 'well they just have to deal with it'. But the point is it means that women are systematically being told that they don't belong, and that does have a cumulative effect. It's also just impractical, you don't want staff struggling with the basics like clothing and where to go to the toilet – they need to be focused on the job in hand. Progress takes time, but it is also worth raising where you see a gap, not just for you but for all others. The thing is, something like that seems pretty innocuous, but it's a very simple way of indicating that you are an outsider – and sort of an annoyance.

I think that time was pretty crucial in teaching me about how important your support can be for another. Time and time again, it was men who had to step forward and take what I said seriously in order for it to be heard or action taken. Sometimes, it was those I least expected who reacted with interest, and looked at ways to improve things, and Nagorno-Karabakh was certainly one of those times.

I used to think the story of the alfresco wee was about me. But it's not at all. It's about all the times someone talks about the difficulties in their experience, and instead of looking at the problem, we look to defend the systems in place, or the motivations of the people involved. This inclination towards self-protection is detrimental to the dismantling of systems of oppression. The defensiveness often stems from the fact that the difficulties faced by those disadvantaged through that system are not considered intentional by those favoured by the system – particularly at an individual level. It is, however, worth remembering how offensive the day-to-day disregard for that person's needs must be, and that the onus is entirely on us to deal with the issue considerately, compassionately, and effectively. There can be sexist or racist elements within groups, organisations, countries, which are not there from ill intent (though some most definitely are). Either way, they must not be upheld, for that compounds the problem. Progress comes from being able to move forward from that criticism.

Training was tough, but I got through it, and came away with the following performance review: 'The programme staff were full of praise for Camilla's approach to training, her ability to listen, understand and to apply what she has learnt. This applies to operations and support training. Camilla's enthusiasm and organisation were commented on by all.' I felt vindicated in so many ways. Actually, one of the most satisfying outcomes came about because I and Susanna (another woman who worked for HALO and later became a friend) completed our operations training there, and as a result the team decided to increase the number of women; there is now an all-female team clearing mines in Nagorno-Karabakh.

For all the emotional strain that Cambodia brought, my time in Nagorno-Karabakh was far more to do with the physical challenge. I wasn't as big or as strong as the men in the Karabakh clearance teams. I knew I would struggle when we were doing our stint in the minefield, and that it was likely that I would be the slowest in the team. When it came to the operations training, however, physical strength and resilience could only get you so far. Actually, in the context of humanitarian work, it really wasn't all about brute strength, but was far more to do with learning about the process, and thus how to manage it safely and effectively. Yes, during training, when I was on my sixth excavation of the morning scraping through frozen ground I wished I was that little bit stronger. Realistically, however, strength and endurance were not the qualities I had that were going to make the greatest difference, so it was about getting through that section of training to the parts I would be good at. I hate not being the best at something, which is part and parcel of being always desperate for approval, so the most painful part of it all for me was the humiliation of being slower. Although I was a lot stronger then than I am now, I also wasn't a six-foot, well-built man. The most important thing that I had to keep in sight was that I didn't need to be. In fact, I was surrounded by them, so perhaps being slightly different could be helpful.

I thoroughly enjoyed the rest of training in Nagorno-Karabakh (in fact, I had also enjoyed the weeks in the minefield in the cold). This included medical training to deal with minefield injuries, and was conducted by a famous war-hero doctor known to have saved many lives during the recent fighting. Everywhere we went with him, people would stop him to shake his hand and thank him for all he had done during the war. His final test for me was to complete a casualty-evacuation exercise, ensuring that I could stabilise and evacuate someone who had suffered a traumatic hand amputation within ten minutes – I managed it in just under nine.

I also completed my first EOD (explosive ordnance disposal) qualification, covering ammunition recognition and disposal, carrying out practice demolitions in a military training ground so close to the front line that I could hear the artillery fire. Our EOD instructor was an older man, as were the majority of my instructors, who favoured what I suppose could be interpreted as a Soviet style of teaching by rote. The lessons were structured to involve a lot of repetition back to him – we were essentially drilled in the information we needed to know, and went over it again and again. This was also partly to do with what we were learning. Recognising weapon types involves committing a lot to memory, learning what markings mean, and how to recognise the different functions. I'm lucky enough to be good at memorising information and then regurgitating at the right moment, so this suited me well – and we were praised if we did well in the tests, which also suited me! In the end, however, I took so much enjoyment from the task that a successful outcome – i.e. doing well in the test – became more a by-product than the focus.

To me this was a crucial lesson, for we live in such a results-oriented world – how many times have we heard the phrase 'If it's not on Instagram it didn't happen'? In doing so, we miss out on the joy of the task. I wanted to pass that course because then I would be able to do a job that I loved, and that I felt was important. I felt no need for extrinsic validation of my choices, because internally I was more than happy with both my decision and the work I was doing. That 'like' for a photo can feel immediately satisfying, but it is fleeting and provides no solid ground for happiness or fulfilment. I never did put a photo on Instagram to say I'd completed my training, but to this day it is one of my proudest accomplishments. It taught me to take that time, and not to necessarily worry too much about the surface appearance of success.

I also learned a valuable lesson about 'image' from my team leader in the minefield, the man who had found me a quiet spot to pee. He would periodically come and stand over me while I worked. Whenever he watched me, I would feel conscious of being slow, and very aware of trying to make sure that I did everything exactly right. He would stand there in silence and I would feel this huge, looming presence; I was extremely intimidated by him. I knew, from the feedback he gave us at the end of each day and from how efficiently he ran the team at the minefield, that he really knew his stuff. I watched him complete a demolition and was in awe of his quiet, calm and controlled demeanour. At the end of my time training in that minefield, we had our photo taken together. It was only when I looked back at the picture that I realised we were actually the same height. He is someone I often think about now. About how he wasn't the loudest, he wasn't the biggest. Nagorno-Karabakh is a fairly macho society, and any macho society has the potential to be difficult for men, who need to fulfil that strong alpha stereotype to be respected. Yet he had complete control of that group, and the respect of every person in it. He reminds me that you can gain respect, even when it is not automatically accorded to you.

That you can be a *presence*, not just a type.

Chapter 3

The Long Drop

————

It's 9 p.m. I'm lying on the camp bed with my head propped on my rolled-up sleeping bag in my tent staring at the 'ceiling'. I love my tent. It's a small dome of tranquillity and calm. It's my space to go away to. Inside, my North Face holdall is lying against one canvas wall. My clothes are sorted in it so that clean clothes are piled closest to my camp bed: one pile of navy HALO T-shirts, one small pile of navy cargo trousers, most with some form of popper missing somewhere, or a little tear on the knee. Pants and socks are tucked in front of the piles. At the other end of the bag are dirty clothes, there's a loose divide along the middle formed by the 'maybe' clothes that are dirty, but clean enough to come in handy should I run out. My day rucksack sits close to my bed, it usually contains my Leatherman and some sun cream as well as some notes from the day. My boots sit at the entrance with socks tucked into them and a head torch strapped round the top, ready in case I need to do a midnight dash to the nearby long drop for a pee.

A long drop is a hole, dug deep into the ground, to be used as a latrine. There's one main rule to a long drop – don't look down. I once had food poisoning in the camp, and went to the long drop. I'm afraid to say that on a hot day, the smell coming up can be quite potent. Usually, it wouldn't bother me much (surprisingly, you get used to it) but on this occasion the smell turned my stomach. As I turned to be sick, I looked down, and the light above illuminated the gloomy depths – and the maggot-filled mass, moving and churning beneath me.

The camp is well established. The other senior staff have dome tents like mine, set out in two long rows, each tent about a metre from the next. Then there is the 'office' tent, where the day's statistics (area cleared in square metres, number of mines destroyed) are radioed back to the HALO headquarters in Harare, Zimbabwe's capital. There's a large medical tent, where the head medic keeps the major-trauma kits that are assigned to each team and taken to the minefield every day in case of any accidents. He also stores various other medicines that may be needed. We are very remote here, as well as off grid, so he is the first port of call for any ailments. Then there are several large tents where the teams of deminers stay, each containing camp beds, sleeping bags and a small amount of space for their belongings.

In the centre of the camp is a large tent that is used for

the demining stores, which also contains the chargers for the batteries that are used in the detectors each day.

Recharging these makes up the bulk of the power requirement for the camp (I know this because when I return to Zimbabwe the following year I am assigned a task to calculate the power usage of the camp to see if we could feasibly move to solar panels). At this time though, the entire camp is run using a 5kVA generator that comes on for a couple of hours in the evening, before everyone goes to bed at around 9 p.m., and an hour in the morning, when the teams are preparing to deploy to the minefields. There are some lightbulbs strung up around the main areas of the camp that allow us to see to pack up the equipment that will be needed for the day's work.

There are a couple of small mud-walled huts, one used as a cold room to store food, the other as a kitchen for preparing the food. Most days we have the same food, beginning with a boiled egg and bread for breakfast. The bread is baked in an outdoor oven in the main camp which is a few kilometres up the road, and each evening we do a bread run there to collect enough for every one of us to take a batch of six small rolls. Most of the staff have a couple in the morning but take the rest with them to the minefield, to snack on during the breaks. The work is extremely physical, even more so in the heat, and needs plenty of sustenance.

Lunch and dinner are usually identical – a spoonful of reconstituted maize meal known as sadza (think Smash but with more of a corn taste). It's served with Zimbabwean leafy greens and either a bean stew, or fresh goat. And yes, by fresh goat, I mean there are a few goats tied to a tree in the camp, that are quietly slaughtered, skinned and butchered, ready to make their way onto our plates for dinner. I know that some people will find this distasteful, but truthfully I found it easier to stomach than the meat industry I was used to in the UK. The goats had been procured from local farmers, providing essential income in a marginalised rural economy, and every single part of the animal was used, so that there was very little waste. I am not a huge fan of goat, and usually keep some tabasco stashed in my bag, but overall the food isn't bad. I quickly become accustomed to the flavours although, without going into too much detail, my digestive tract takes a bit longer to get used to the sadza.

The 'toilet' and 'shower' are two small structures in the corner of the camp. The floor of each is a small block of cement surrounding a hole, and the walls are built up using sticks cut from the surrounding bush at each corner, covered by black tarpaulin and large, dry leaves, leaving the top open. Of these, one is the aforementioned long drop, the other is where you can take a bucket of water and wash away the day's dust and dirt. I actually love bucket showers, and usually leave my bucket of water out warming in the sun during the day. Then, just as the sun goes down, I wander over to the shower block, wet my soap a little, rub it all over myself, including my hair, and then empty half the bucket over my head. It is the best sensation to feel the dust washed from my body as the heat is going out of the fiery, orange sun, and the wild African bushland behind the shower is plunged into darkness all along a spectacular skyline.

The only problem is the short walk between my tent and the shower hut. There are only about six female deminers with HALO in Zimbabwe at this time, and they are all based in another camp further along the border with Mozambique. I worry about the appropriate thing to wear on the walk from my tent to the shower. I like to change into something clean after I've showered as my day clothes are always caked in dust, but wearing my kit over there, as well as carrying my bucket of water, bar of soap, towel and a full set of clean clothes nearly always ends in my losing half my warm water all over the dry clothes I mean to change into. Then, of course, there is the fear that, once I'm in the shower hut, someone will mistakenly come in.

The worst is when one evening I reach the shower cubicle and strip off, only to find I have dropped my soap somewhere on the way. I can't work out whether to get fully dressed again to go out and look for it. And should I take all my stuff? What if someone comes to take a shower and finds my clean pants hanging over the side of the cubicle? It sounds ridiculous but it would feel uncomfortable for my belongings to be found – I would feel awkward, but more than that, I know the person who found them would also feel awkward. In the end, I nip out in my T-shirt as quickly as I can, keeping one eye on the entrance to the cubicle, and luckily find the soap a few metres from the entrance, dropped in a little pile of goat dung. I figure out a system over the coming weeks, perfecting my 'shower pile' and carrying arrangement, but I am still envious of the guys wandering around comfortably in their shorts, with towels slung over their bare shoulders.

The programme here is extremely well run. Zimbabwe is one of the very best places to work and train for a number of reasons. Firstly, nearly everyone speaks English – as much as this doesn't always sit well with me (a reminder of Zimbabwe's turbulent history), it is nice to be able to communicate a bit more directly than when doing so through an interpreter. Even in terms of work, it is a relief to know exactly what is being said rather than relying on a translator. Beyond that, it gives me the opportunity to get to know a bit more about the people I work with, to share those scraps of humour that surface during a working day, and which wouldn't always be translated for me in other places. It seems such an obvious thing to be missing, and yet is something that perhaps I hadn't realised that I had missed before. Many moments of kinship come from conversations over making a cup of tea, or as you grumble together about another early start. There is so much in those details, so much that you learn about people from the quips they make about the talk your boss has just given. So much that helps you find 'your' people, the ones with whom you have most in common. So much that teaches you which person to ask to do a particular task. There is a language that I was missing, too, that I didn't realise I was: friendly terms that make you feel part of a group and included.

The other significant advantage is that the majority of the senior HALO staff are drawn from those recruited by the commercial demining companies that had sprung up since the early nineties. Many of the HALO Zimbabwe staff have completed contracts in the Falklands or Afghanistan and that experience came with both a wealth of technical knowledge, and valuable insight into the practicalities of mine clearance. Things like how to manage and deploy teams, how to run camps, how to plan operations, how to keep track of equipment – all the aspects of running operations that are so essential. They had often worked with members of various militaries, and their attention to detail and standards of organisation were exceptional. Each morning we would parade in front of the tents for roll call, and then a member of the team would lead a prayer. The time this started depended mainly on seasonal variations: the hotter the weather got, the earlier the working day started. It ranged between 4:20 and 5 a.m. The staff were committed to maintaining standards, and frequently used these morning parades to retest staff on the standard operating procedures (SOPs).

I arrived to complete the second phase of my operations training (having passed the first stage in Nagorno-Karabakh), and this depth of knowledge amongst the senior staff means that I'm learning a lot very quickly. My days are happily busy. I'm still technically training, having moved into Phase 2, but a lot of my skills from my role as projects officer in Cambodia will start to come into play, for I will learn more about the programme-management side of things.

The first thing I need to do, however, is spend some time working as a deminer in the minefields that were laid by the

Rhodesian forces during the Liberation War in the 1970s.[5] Zimbabwe is one of the most mined countries in the world, and the borders with Mozambique and Zambia are lined with dense minebelts. These belts are of a recognisable structure, so much so that it's relatively easy to predict where a mine will be. In fact, the pattern is so predictable that there is a 'missed mine drill' for cases when a device is not found where expected. The mines are South African-made R2M2s. Cylindrical, and measuring about 6 cm high by 7 cm wide, they are still largely functional despite having been laid in the late 1970s.

The challenges here are different from those in Nagorno-Karabakh. There the soil was frozen solid, but here it is sun baked until it's as hard as cement. Occasionally one of the supervisors will come along with a watering can and soften up an area where a deminer is completing an excavation. And the plastic-bodied mines, the South African R2M2s, contain minimum metal, and so are very difficult to find with a detector. We are using Minelab detectors, with the sensitivity settings increased to account for this, but unfortunately this means that we are receiving false signals from mineralised soil, complicating and slowing clearance efforts. In basic terms, we are conducting a lot of extra excavations because there is no way the detectors can distinguish between a metal

---

[5] The Zimbabwe Liberation Struggle is also known as the Second Chimurenga or the Rhodesian Bush War. It lasted from July 1964 to 1979, and resulted in the end of white-minority rule in Rhodesia, and the creation of the Republic of Zimbabwe. It involved conflict between Ian Smith's government, and Robert Mugabe's Zimbabwe African National Union and Joshua Nkomo's Zimbabwe African People's Union. Smith was a dedicated advocate for white rule. The civil struggle was to achieve independence for Zimbabwe, and the freedom to form a government elected democratically by Zimbabwe's population.

signal and a false signal. You only know when the signal disappears as you excavate and you find it was caused by a little bit of dirt that you then put it in your bucket – perhaps the least satisfying task but entirely necessary, as it could be masking a real signal.

In Zimbabwe, they are trying to counter this problem by using dual-detectors that also have ground-penetration radar (GPR), the idea being that this searches around the metal signal for a body that looks like a mine. The detectors we are using are HSTAMIDS, an acronym for Handheld Standoff Mine Detection System. HALO's are from NVESD, the US Army's Night Vision and Electronic Sensors Directorate. In return for the detectors, detailed statistics of their performance are passed back to NVESD in monthly reports from HALO's Research and Development projects manager.

Using them is relatively complex. They are heavy and unwieldy. There is a very specific scanning motion that has to be completed in order to get a correct reading back. The teams are currently conducting red chip/blue chip drills. The red and blue chips are made from little painted circles of wood, about 2 cm in diameter. In brief, the HSTAMIDS operator goes along what is known as a 'bound'. The bound in mine clearance terms is a strip of land that is currently uncleared, which adjoins the currently cleared land, and is marked to be cleared next. A deminer has already marked with a red chip any signals that have been found using a Minelab detector. The HSTAMIDS operator conducts a search over each red chip the Minelab operator has laid. If the HSTAMIDS detector indicates that there *is* a body around the metal signal, indicating that there may be a mine hidden beneath the soil, the operator leaves the red chip in place. If it looks as though it may be a nuisance signal, such as from a discarded bottle cap, the operator replaces the red chip with a blue one.

Once the drill has been confirmed to be working – that is, the operators are correctly marking clutter signals, and not landmines, with blue chips – rapid excavation techniques can be used at the blue-chip sites. In Cambodia, they used a device known as a 'clutternator', so called because it is designed to filter out metal clutter signals. It is an adapted strimmer, which the operator uses to rapidly dig a hole of the requisite depth to check if a mine is there. To use rapid excavation techniques you have to be confident that you are not excavating down on top of a mine. So, over the first months of their use, you collect data about the HSTAMIDS. There are two crucial pieces of information you need to gather. Firstly, the number of mines miscalled, or put another way, the number of mines labelled as blue chips that should be red chips. Ideally this number is zero. Secondly, you record the clutter rejection rate, which is the number of signals that can be disregarded or labelled as clutter, meaning the site can be rapidly excavated. This rate indicates how much you have been able to improve efficiency through successfully marking clutter signals with blue chips.

The catch in all this is that there are only a certain number of the devices available, and it takes time and effort to train staff on them. They have already been shown to work well in other long-standing HALO countries, like Cambodia, but

HALO Zimbabwe is still really in its infancy and so the use of HSTAMIDS, as well as other dual-detectors, is still being integrated into the programme. In time, this will provide gains in productivity, but it takes a while to get the system set up properly.

Another challenge for the Zimbabwe programme is that the country's military also currently bans humanitarian operators from using explosives to dispose of mines (this is no longer the case today). The safest way to neutralise a mine, once located, is to set a donor charge next to it and blow it up. It's much less risky than fiddling around trying to defuse a device that has potentially been compromised over the years it has spent buried beneath the earth. In Zimbabwe, we don't have that luxury. Instead, the mines need to be carefully excavated until they can be lifted. They are then carried in a bucket of soil to a small prepared bunker to be stored until the end of the day, when they are placed on small, individual wire boxes – basically, tiny barbecues upon which the mines can be burnt. These boxes are known as 'HOBBs', which stands for high-order burning boxes, and provide an alternative to destroying the mines in-situ using explosives, by incinerating the mine until it explodes. They are lined up and one of the supervisors goes along the line, lighting each burner before retreating to the safe area, from where usually you hear a series of pops as each mine detonates; it is advisable to keep track of these pops to ensure the expected number explode.

As part of my training, I complete the excavation and lifting drill. Lifting is not something that is encouraged, for there are obvious risks associated with digging around a mine – particularly old ones that have been subject to various forces over the time they have spent in the ground. There have been a few occasions in Zimbabwe when mines have low-ordered as they were excavated or lifted by HALO staff. A low-order or partial detonation happens when there is incomplete detonation of a high explosive, usually caused by a physical break or lack of chemical homogeneity within the explosive material. Essentially, wear and tear may have damaged the mine, but although this damage may mean the mine does not function properly, resulting in a much smaller (low-order) explosion, it also means the mine may become more likely to detonate prematurely if disturbed. Although the majority of the mines in Zimbabwe continue to function as intended, some may have experienced considerable damage, which in turn has reduced their stability, and also their functionality. A low-order detonation may still cause injury though, including but not limited to, the loss of a finger. Great care and precision are needed. Basically, we only lift mines because we absolutely have to, and if there was another option (like the use of explosives) we would take it.

I am lucky (or unlucky, as you may look at it) that the HALO programme manager is there to guide me through the lifting drill for the first time. This tells you a lot about how I react to authority; I am much more worried about getting it wrong in front of him than I am about, say, losing a finger or something. That is embarrassing, but true. I lie flat on my front, my face about 30 centimetres away from the mine.

Usually when you are carrying out a normal excavation you sit up on your knees; that way your body armour shields your vital organs should the mine go off, while the visor protects your face, deflecting the blast away from you. When carrying out this more intensive excavation, however, you usually lie in the prone position, flat on your front on the ground. In general, it is a more comfortable position from which to get right in and around the mine, and does offer protection in that you are outside of the blast zone.

Usually you start with the larger scraper, exposing as much of the mine as you safely can, and then you carry on with a smaller tool that resembles a screwdriver. You slowly loosen the soil underneath and to the sides of the mine. You need it to stay in place because if it tips out and over into the excavation pit it could fall face down and go off. Equally, you need to loosen the soil enough that you can gently lift the device out – you can't be tugging it out as you could make contact between the pressure plate on top and the soil, exerting enough pressure on the top plate of the mine for it to go off.

I am carefully excavating when I hit something more solid than soil. I work around to the other side and discover the same. I realise there is a narrow tree root that has grown around the mine, and as I clear more soil away, I can see part of the root rests on the top pressure plate. This is not ideal! I start using my secateurs to clip away parts of the root, being careful not to release the mine completely from its woody grasp. On my hands I'm wearing what are to all intents and purposes large gardening gloves. That may sound ludicrous, but they have actually been shown to offer good protection against blast. The only problem is that they are on the big side for me. I have tiny hands, and although the gloves are the smallest size available, there is still a fair amount of excess stiff material. Additionally, mine are slightly clogged with wet soil, from an earlier excavation when I had used water to soften the earth.

My dexterity's usually relatively good, and I am trying to work as delicately as possible. I focus on what I can and can't see. Reaching out, I gently test whether the mine is free enough to lift away. It's not. I could sense my boss looming over me, and I desperately wanted to show confidence in his explanation of the process, as well as in my own abilities. Care and precision are always stressed, and he had been very clear to me to take my time, but equally it is important not to take too long to complete a straightforward task. Gently, I loosen a bit more of the soil, and reach out and test the mine and this time it comes away. The root is still attached, holding together soil on top of the mine. I carefully place it in a bucket of soil and carry it to the safety area, accompanied by the programme manager.

He is well known in HALO, one of the longest-serving staff. He has a reputation for being exceptionally knowledgeable, but also for being an extremely balanced and fair boss. He worked for HALO in the early years, which were far riskier. They were still learning about clearance, but riskier still was the fact that they were often the first boots on the ground in some of the worst-affected conflict areas. Their imperative was to reach the people who needed them as soon as they possibly could. They would find a way into the area, and hit the ground running, setting up headquarters, recruiting staff and working out ways to get the equipment they needed into the country. There is a long-standing joke that each country office used to just have a fax machine, and periodically these would send one sheet to the headquarters in Scotland reading 'Send more money'!

When I think now about what they did in the early days, I am in awe. I found it hard enough to drop into a ready-made established programme, with security awareness and risk assessments already in place. There were still new programmes being set up, but we were in a different era of HALO, in which support is well established, and I had much to learn from those who had sharpened their sense of risk and developed considerable mental robustness within the chaotic environments of HALO's early years.

While we are over at the small explosives store putting away the mine I have lifted to be burned at the end of the day with any other mines found, he shows me a MAPS mine, another type of pressure-operated anti-personnel mine, which are found buried in the ground. They have an interesting explosive chain, with a detonator located in the side of the device. He shows me how to locate the small cap on the outside that indicates where the detonator has been slid into a thin tube. He asks me if I'd like to try to take one out.

So I take out my Leatherman and open one of the blades. The mine is old and dirty, time has melded the cap into its plastic coating, and finding the seam isn't a simple task. I hold the device firmly in my left hand, with the pressure plate facing away from me. The sweat drips down my face into my eyes. I'd just taken my hair down as my ponytail had somehow wound itself around the rear band of my visor, pulling the visor backwards uncomfortably. Now my hair feels hot on my neck, the sun is beaming down and I see it reflect off my blade. I am so HOT, and my visor is claustrophobic. I take a few deep, cooling breaths, but the warm, moist air I breathe out is trapped in front of my face. It's funny how all the things your body would normally tolerate suddenly become magnified through the lens of an irritating task. I suppose it's not really irritating, it's just painstaking and requires concentration.

The mine is still in full working order, so great care is required. Eventually I ease the cap off, and very gently tip the detonator into my hand. The detonator is what triggers an explosive device – they are therefore, by nature and design, very sensitive. Detonators are always handled with care, for even though the amount of explosives they contain is very small, if one were to explode in your hand it would definitely cost you a few digits. Extracting a detonator leaves the main charge in the body of the mine, and breaks the chain that is required to initiate the detonation of the more stable main-charge explosives. I hold the base of the detonator between my forefinger and thumb and beam up at my boss, who luckily snapped a photo. I say 'luckily' because it wasn't usual to take pictures, really, and it happened only because I had taken my camera out to the minefield that day to get some good clearance photos for donor reports. But, happily, I do have that moment captured. I am sweaty and red-faced, and look unashamedly proud. It really was not much of an achievement, but in that moment I had one task to do, and that's what I did. Life is simpler when you have one task, when you just have something in front of you that you need to complete. I know that was part of the reason why I found that work so satisfying.

That, and the tangibility of it all, of being able actually to do something valuable in an area where the effects of mines were so very clear. Many of the local villages are cut off from facilities on the other side of this extensive border minefield, like schools and health centres. Where we are working many children are using paths through the minefields to walk to school, or taking massive two-hour detours to make what should be a short journey. The area should be used for grazing cattle, on which family livelihoods depend, and over 100,000 cattle have been injured or killed in mine accidents. These are huge risks for families to take, although it is not always that clear cut; many areas aren't fenced and cattle will make their own way to the tasty, tempting treat that minefields present – their lack of cultivation allowing grass, shrubs and patches to flourish. If people or cattle stray into the minefield we have to pause work – it simply isn't safe to continue. Cattle, in particular, are liable to wander into uncleared areas, and are more than heavy enough to apply the pressure required to initiate a landmine (it is a real tragedy when they do, not only for the animal that suffers, but because they are valuable assets and the loss of or injury to a cow can have a serious impact on a family's livelihood).

The paths are cleared first, the ones that will be most widely used, but the swaths of contaminated land are extensive, and these are communities that have been isolated for a long time. Their desperation has led them to try to establish their own 'safe' routes. But while the local knowledge is extensive, it all too often becomes apparent that it only takes a slight side step, 5 cm off the footprint made yesterday, for someone to become a casualty.

If current estimates are correct, there are many more landmines in Zimbabwe than in Afghanistan, and these are affecting the very poorest of communities living in the border regions. The presence of mines threatens life and limb, and those who have already suffered accidents are not in a position to afford, or even access, prosthetics. HALO works with a local provider of prosthetic limbs, arranging times for him to meet survivors of mine accidents in our camps and fit them for new limbs. Some of the older prosthetics that have been issued are woefully inadequate. They look terrible, are ill-fitting, badly made and uncomfortable, and so many of those suffering are also those who are reliant on their physical ability to survive. Livelihoods in this area mainly depend on farming and cross-border trade. Many of the local HALO staff come from these villages, and talk often about the effect of mines on the daily lives of landmine victims – about their restricted access to water, latrines, and, of course, agricultural land.

The one thing no one will talk about, or at least no one does in front of me, is politics. It is 2015, Mugabe retained power in the 2013 elections but was widely accused of electoral fraud. Before travelling here, I read two memoirs of life in Zimbabwe, *When a Crocodile Eats the Sun* by Peter Godwin and *Don't Let's Go to the Dogs Tonight* by Alexandra Fuller, hoping to glean some kind of understanding of the history of the country. As much as the history of Zimbabwe's minefields, with which we are provided as part of our training materials, gives a good insight into the history of the conflict, it is often described in relation to work, as in which sides laid landmines, where, when and why. The purpose of such information is to help inform clearance strategy, so the text is prosaic and unsurprisingly pragmatic. I had seen Zimbabwe mentioned enough on the news as I was growing up, however, to know that there was a depth and complexity to this history, and to realise that it would be disrespectful not to try to develop some kind of understanding of how it came about. As I understood it, I did not come from a nation blameless in the troubles Zimbabwe has faced.

When we learn about places, people, conflicts, anything really, from afar, there is a sense of detachment, no matter how good we may be at putting ourselves in someone else's shoes, so much of a country's history is tied into things that can't be articulated, or not, at least, in a news report. There are feelings, mannerisms, attitudes with roots in personal experience or long-held beliefs, or in relationships between families. It is remarkable how it is the most ordinary things that become ineffable, yet it is those fragments of daily reality that hold together the pieces of history. So, you can know the apparent facts, and some of those with regards to Zimbabwe are dreadfully uncomfortable truths. You can know who governed and when, and perhaps even why, and that is what I knew before I went there, a few facts about a country. That was one level of truth. But when I arrived in Zimbabwe I fell in love with a place I had not known existed. It is one of the strangest feelings I've experienced, because it's the first place where my feet have hit the ground that has felt so instantly like home.

Introversion vs. Extroversion

However, this world, that I fell quite naturally into in many ways not just in terms of a shared language, but also a genuine affinity with and love for the country itself, also highlighted how different I feel I am, and that brings me back to lying in my tent looking up at its roof. I loved that tent, not just because I was happy at the end of day's work to go and lie down there and fall into the deepest of sleeps, but also because I do like to be on my own, and I particularly value having time to reflect in privacy in the evening. It wasn't the physical work I found exhausting, but learning how the social aspect worked. Trying to understand the right cues, to calculate when to say something and when to shut up. I dreaded saying anything that was wrong or, worse, rude (though inadvertently), in a group of people for whom I felt considerable respect.

A part of me wondered about the role gender disparity played, and I will come to that later. A lot of the time, though, I agonised about my own individual shortcomings. I had now seen enough of the world, both inside and outside

HALO, to understand that a certain type of person most often impresses and succeeds in a number of fields, and that person is the extrovert. We struggle to reconcile ideas of strength and sensitivity, and I found that disconcerting. That because I was quiet, or even small, I was assumed incapable not only of physical strength, but also of mental strength. I would be the first to say I feel things strongly and tend to react emotionally, but this ability to empathise is what motivates me. In fear of showing what was considered a weakness, I became very good at showing no emotion at all. Indeed, I may have swung too far in the other direction, not even showing a proportional emotional response to anything.

This was not necessarily a good thing. To have learned to fear showing my emotions was to have reached a point where I smothered one of my strengths, simply because others saw it as weak, or at least, I thought they did. However much I felt pressured to put on a brave face, I should have set boundaries. I should have found ways to exist as myself. Instead I started to sacrifice parts of my identity, in a bid to form a new one: one that would fit the bill, one that would make up for what I lacked in terms of physical strength. Rather than embrace what made me different, I made every attempt to become the same – to fit in, and where my genetics would not allow this, I was plunged into ever deeper self-loathing.

I should admit here that I am naturally prone to introversion. I am shy and sensitive, and although I do have a fun side, I certainly come across as serious – and it would be accurate to say that this is how I approach most aspects of life. I was aware that many of the problems I felt speaking up within groups and addressing authority were to do with my character, but I do think this feeling that I needed to change was compounded by some aspects of gender disparity. I found that in nearly every place I worked women and men were treated differently. I don't mean this in the way of calling out my former colleagues, but we were working in long-established systems that made it inevitable that culturally it was less normal for a woman to be included in certain types of discussions, and unusual for one to speak up or to take control of a situation.

So, it is perhaps easy for someone to tell me that I was too introverted, that I should have spoken up more, that I should have been more assertive. However, on the occasions when I tried this I often found that I got a more immediate negative result. For example, in Cambodia I would ask for a particular task to be done and someone would agree but it just wouldn't get done. It wasn't outright insubordination, it was inherent bias leading to less respect. As a result, I spent a lot more time following up, and relatively easy tasks became more complex and time-consuming.

I often found I had to ask people in a gentler way to do the same tasks in order to avoid annoying anyone – consequently, on occasions, I would be told by my male non-local counterparts that I needed to be more assertive or authoritative. But that was straightforward for them in a way that it wasn't for me, as a woman. It's hard for me to be objective here, but I think I did try over the years in many of the places I worked, and found it could be ineffective because socially it jarred. In Cambodia, I had an occasion where I was discussing something serious with a member of staff, and halfway through he mimed batting me away with his hand in my face, rolled his eyes and walked off. I did know that wouldn't have happened with a man, but I also spent a lot more time reflecting on what I could have done differently in that conversation to make it work for him.

On my way to Zimbabwe, I'd been asked to take a suitcase of HALO items (it was not unusual to be asked to hand-carry some items out to a programme), in addition to my own bag. I had all the necessary documents, as well as the cash to pay the customs fee, and it shouldn't have been a problem. Yet, as my bags were scanned through on arrival in Harare airport, an official took me aside, and repeatedly told me that I wouldn't be allowed through unless we made some kind of 'deal'. The tones were definitely overtly sexual, as opposed to being related to money. I stood my ground, and repeatedly mentioned that I had someone waiting to collect me on the other side who would be questioning where I was. The official became more disgruntled, and the arrivals hall emptied, leaving me and one other woman, who was trying to negotiate her way out of paying a fee to bring in second-hand clothing donations for children. The need for a 'deal to be made' was mentioned again, and even that there was a private customs room where the 'deal' could be discussed further. I declined, and suggested that if there was a problem with the paperwork or the fee that had been paid, they had all the details of the charity, and the address should they wish to follow up for further payment. Eventually, they let me through, and I met my programme manager on the other side, who asked how it had gone because I had taken longer than expected. I explained about this need to make a 'deal', but I felt too ashamed and embarrassed to mention how uncomfortable the situation had been, and how it had seemed sexual in nature. I felt awkward that I hadn't been able to complete a very basic task, without it becoming a hassle. Customs can be tricky in Zimbabwe, but I think for any of my male counterparts the issues would have been related to money, and I was concerned with there being a stigma attached to my suggesting that I had experienced anything otherwise.

Maybe I had swung too much in the opposite direction and should have been a bit more assertive; perhaps there was a middle ground that I hadn't managed to find. Part of my way of thinking is the result of moving through countries where the social dynamics are all different, which tends to affect men less as they are invariably top of the pecking order. Attitudes to women vary wildly from country to country, however, and so I was trying to find my management style in circumstances that were not consistent.

During my time in Zimbabwe, I would hear frequently senior male staff discussing the six female deminers and comparing their work productivity to that of their male counterparts. Looking at a deminer's productivity is very straightforward: it's to do with the area they are managing to clear per day, taking into account the average clearance rates on their minefield. The six women's productivity was being compared to the productivity of over a hundred male staff. Of course, it was being averaged per person, but taking a minority and comparing it with a majority is never a fair way of doing things, not least because it doesn't take into account any of the unique challenges they might be facing. The idea was that if those women couldn't keep up with the men, then they weren't going to be an asset in getting clearance done as quickly as possible, and therefore, they adjudged, there was sufficient evidence that no more female staff should be recruited. This is not a fair way of doing things, and not only did I take issue with it at the time, but it also seeped into my own attitude to myself and my work. I felt I had a greater responsibility to demonstrate my use and value as a representative of women, and to deal with challenges without complaint, in order to avoid being a bad representative.

On top of this, I didn't really have an archetype to work from. There wasn't a woman I could look to, or ask advice from. I often found that my male counterparts felt equipped to advise me when they weren't necessarily experiencing the same issues. This, of course, goes both ways, but I did not feel that there was really a need for me to offer advice to them, or at least I was never asked. There is a lot to be said for being sent into the unknown and trying to find your own path. But at times I felt as though I was drowning. I felt like I spent my days trying to assimilate information, only to end the day feeling more confused than ever.

My younger brother gave me some of the best advice I have ever had while I wrestled with this dilemma, which I am talking about here but which really spanned all my years with HALO; indeed, if I'm completely honest it is something

I still think about now. He told me, 'Just keep saying clever things. Keep saying the right things at the right times. Keep asking the right questions. People start to hear this, and you build the circle of people who trust you. Who want to know your opinion. As you build credibility, you build up the circle of people who respect you, and slowly isolate those who don't want to listen to you simply because of who you are and what you represent.'

I will admit that I felt some vindication when I received my training evaluation. As much as the programme in Zimbabwe was well run, it is always worth questioning the status quo in such environments, and despite my reticence, I did speak up about any inefficiencies I saw. Each country programme is, by virtue of geography, isolated, so a lot of the transfer of institutional knowledge happens through the movement of staff. Each time I raised a point, there would be one or two people who would slap it down. Despite this, I carried on raising the issues, although I found myself excusing what I was about to say before I said it, or trying to say it in a gentler manner. When I left, the programme manager gave me the following review:

Camilla has been the strongest of the trainees to come through the programme and it was clear that she has learned a great amount during her admin time in Cambodia. She is quick to pick things up (ops, admin, technical) and impressed with her existing data/GIS knowledge. She is very self-deprecating but her points are always worth listening to. She will be an asset on any programme and could probably move into location management very easily.

I was grateful to him for allowing me to try to establish myself as a credible voice within a team. I think that had he jumped into the discussions, even if in support of my point, it would have undermined my voice. Instead, he allowed me to claim my place in that world. When I arrived in Zimbabwe I was referred to by the local staff as 'miss'; by the time I left I was 'ma'am'. Whether this was because my fair Scottish skin aged rapidly from unaccustomed sun exposure is unclear. I hope it had more to do with me building skills and confidence – yet I can't deny that I still don't fully know how to claim my rightful space, or that when I reflect on my time with HALO, I still find myself frustrated and confused as to what I got right and what I got wrong.

Chapter 4

Misfire

In October 2015, I completed an advanced explosive ordnance disposal qualification, alongside around twelve other HALO employees. I travelled back to Nagorno-Karabakh for three weeks' intensive training to become certified as an IMAS[6] Level 3 Practitioner. The subjects covered by the course are as follows: Explosive Theory; Land Service Ammunition; Landmines and Booby Traps; Air-Dropped Weapons; Guided Weapons; Storage, Transportation and Handling of Explosives; Management of Demolition Sites; Demolitions; Battle Area Clearance; Threat Assessment and Planning; and EOD Task Management.

My mother was not pleased. It was her sixtieth birthday that year, and for months I had had two weeks of annual

---

[6] The International Mine Action Standards (IMAS) are the standards in force for all UN mine action operations. Initially endorsed by the UN Inter-Agency Coordination Group on Mine Action in 2001, the IMAS have remained a cornerstone of all mine action field interventions for over seventeen years.

leave booked in October to attend the celebrations. She and Dad were going to drive all the way down from Scotland, as they had organised a dinner in London to make it easier for everyone to attend. Then one day I opened my work email to find the dates for the course had been sent out and, of course, they exactly coincided with Mum's birthday. There was no way to have them changed: attendees for the course come from HALO programmes all over the world, and it takes a huge effort to coordinate plans from all these different country programmes. Nor could I miss the course, for that would significantly affect my future opportunities. I had moved countries at this point, from Zimbabwe, then to Georgia, and on to Mozambique, but to his credit, the desk officer who had originally approved my leave dates apologised for the clash, which was unexpected but appreciated. I called my mum and broke the news, and I knew exactly how disappointed she was. This was to have been the first time all the family would be together, cousins whom I hadn't seen for years, aunts and uncles, my brother and sisters. And I wasn't going to be there.

I felt uneasy about the course, too. I found the idea of being in a large group intimidating. First of all, you are usually separated from your peers in the organisation because if you are of equivalent experience, you are unlikely to be placed in the same country. HALO runs a lean expatriate structure, and there is usually no need for several people of the same experience level in one country. We were all going to be in the same accommodation and sharing rooms. I don't know why – it may be from my early days of boarding school, where I didn't really fit in – but anything like that triggers anxiety in me. I can't help but think that I'm going to be the one whom no one wants around. It tends to make me even quieter and more serious than I usually am, and that creates a self-fulfilling prophecy as I appear stand-offish, which in turn makes it hard for anyone to strike up a conversation with me.

Very happily, I am not the only woman on the course. Since I joined HALO a couple of years previously, the organisation has worked hard at increasing the number of women employed by them, with the result that there are three other women in a group of about twelve people.

Susanna, one of the other women, bought a small kettle, and every evening a few of us would make our way to a local shop and buy lemon, fresh ginger, honey and lots of snacks. All four of us were in a room together, and would spend a lot of time revising together. In particular, Susanna and I would go through our presentations together, which we have to do while on the course. It's a presentation regarding the programme in the country where we are currently based. It is nothing to do with passing the course, it's just because it is unusual to have so many of us in the same place, and so a good opportunity to share information. We often practise ours together, Susanna and I, performing them for each other and pointing out areas for improvement. Neither of us is keen on speaking in public. On the day, I look straight out as I begin my presentation and catch sight of her friendly face. Later she tells me that she could see me grinning at her throughout her whole talk. This memory is one of my very strongest from my time with HALO, and while it may not sound like a lot, moments like this are important for me. Until that point I had not realised how lonely I was feeling in HALO, and a moment of solidarity like that was comforting.

Beyond the presentation, in order to pass the course, there are a number of written and practical exams. The first was a recognition and identification test. You walk around a room filled with FFE items of unexploded ordnance (UXO) and work out what they are, the risk they pose, and if you were disposing of them, where you would put the donor charges, to ensure they are completely destroyed. We also have to take an hour-long written exam, before completing the practical tests that include both electrical and non-electrical demolition drills, and demonstration of the correct misfire protocols. There is also a practical test known as 'EOD task scene management'. For this three instructors set up a different scenario for each of us. On entering this you have to decide the appropriate way to deal with the situation. They are checking that you correctly identify the item, and then establish the correct follow-up drill, such as calculating how many sandbags you'll need.

Before we start our practical training, we complete the aforementioned hour-long written exam. Written exams are something I can do. I am still extremely nervous before sitting one, and I always come out of the exam convinced that I've done badly, but if I'm honest, I have the learning style and memory that are suited to written exams. One morning, as we are all loading the trucks for the day out at the training ground, one of the instructors comes around with a notebook telling each person their result for the written test. Just as I am collecting items from the store, he heads my way, and gives me my result; I came top with 98 per cent. So really, I *know* what I am doing, but practical tests always hold more fear for me. I find the process of doing something in front of someone intimidating. When I complete the drills on my own, I feel extremely comfortable, even in a risky situation. It's just the idea of being watched that I can't handle. In the event, the first few practical tests go absolutely fine. After each, I heave a sigh of relief and wonder what I had worried about.

I am probably most worried about the safety-fuse test, not because it is harder than any of the others but mainly because how you've performed is very visible. For the most part, when you are conducting demolitions, you use electrical initiation to detonate the charge because it gives you greater control. You don't initiate the demolition until you have returned to the firing point – a safe distance from the item that is to be demolished. This is usually the preferred method, but there are instances where it is not appropriate, such as underneath electrical pylons which may cause electrical interference, making the process risky. In those cases, safety fuse is used.

The first thing you do is burn a 30-cm length of safety fuse to determine the burn time, which should be between 35 and 50 seconds. You then time the walk from the disposal area to the safe area, and then, very importantly, you double that time. Then you calculate how much fuse is required to allow that time. You double it just in case something goes wrong, which is your buffer to allow for tripping up or other mishaps – anything that slows your return to the safety area. This is because once you have lit the safety fuse, there is no way of stopping the explosion. You have to be outside the area by the time the charge goes off.

When you've done your calculations and cut the required length of safety fuse, you take a detonator out of your det box, and crimp it on to one end of the fuse. It's a good idea to cut this end completely square, so that it fits snugly into the detonator, while it is best to cut the other end on a slant (known as a scarfed cut), which makes it easier to light with a match. This is because you have to light the fuse and start your stopwatch at exactly the same time. The easiest way to do this is to balance the end of the match against the slant-cut end of the safety fuse, and then strike it with the rough edge of the matchbox. This gives you a cleaner light, and it's easier to start your watch at the same time.

You walk to the item with your prepared safety fuse and det, and a block of TNT, the so-called 'donor charge'. You carefully place the donor charge as close to the item as you can without touching it, fit the detonator into the block – we are using TNT blocks and most already have a hole in which to slot the detonator, and lay out the safety fuse – you may need to use small pegs like the metal pegs that come with tents to ensure it is spread out flat. Finally, you light the other end of the safety fuse and at exactly the same time you start your stopwatch, check you've got all your equipment with you, and walk back to the firing point. Just before the 10-second point, you request quiet to those around you and over the radio, and then start the countdown, calling out loud: '9 8 7 6 5 4 3 2 1 BANG 1 2 3 4 5 6 7 8 9 10'.

So long as the bang happens within that 10-second window either side of zero, you pass the test. The point, however, is that for that to happen, everything needs to have been done right: the timing of the safety fuse burn, the calculations of the length of fuse required, the cutting of each end of the fuse, starting the stopwatch at exactly the same time as you light the fuse. There are so many mistakes you could have made at some point in the process. I remember once watching someone in Zimbabwe count past 'BANG' all the way back up to ten and then beyond with a desperate look on his face. It turned out that he had accidentally cut an extra 10 cm of fuse – and all I could think was 'What an easy mistake to make.' The incident had haunted me ever since.

We have been divided into groups during the safety fuse test, but there are still people who have already finished their tests and are standing next to the firing point, chatting. All of them will be thinking about their own test, but in my narcissistic mind, I feel that they are all watching me. Also, I do know that I can sometimes come across as a little Miss Know-It-All. It is not at all how I feel inside, but it's what I project. I have a good memory, and am often able to repeat back verbatim what I have been taught in a class. It doesn't make me any better at the practical side of the work, it's just something I am able to do, and I think I feel added pressure because I have done well in the written exam. I have often seen people take great delight in my getting something wrong, and it always puts me on edge, feeling as though I am for ever on the precipice of making a fool of myself.

I look at my stopwatch, and feel a cold anxiety clutch at my chest. The countdown I have calculated is getting closer, I begin to panic that I have even got that wrong and that I'm confused about when I should start counting. 'Calm down, calm down' I say over and over to myself. At the moment I have calculated I call out: 'Quiet, firing! 9 8 7 6 5 4 3 2 1...' BANG! – the charge goes off! I go forward and do the demolition site checks, and then the instructor, Zarif, shakes my hand. I walk back to the group and Susanna instantly congratulates me, a huge smile on her face.

On the following day, we are individually called in to a room with the three course instructors, and given our reports. I hate talks like these, because however good the result, they make me feel uncomfortable and awkward. I'm one of the last to be called in. The instructors are very complimentary, but I can't take it in. Although I never know how to react to bad news, I never know how to react to good news either.

A few weeks later, by which time I have travelled on to HALO Mozambique, I decide to email Zarif to thank him. He is Afghan, and one of the most experienced EOD instructors you could hope to meet, and I wanted to say thank you for everything he had taught me. I still have those e-mails and his response is below (I should add, in case anyone thinks I am mocking him, that his English is a great deal better than my Dari or Pashto).

Misfire

Zarif,

I hope this finds you well.

I just wanted to send you an email to say thank you for all your help and instruction during the EOD 2 course. It was a privilege to meet you and to have the opportunity to learn from you. Many thanks for all the time and effort you put into making the course a success.

Kind regards,
Camilla

And his reply:

Dear Camilla

Thanks I'm doing well... And hope the same for you. Thanks for your email and this shows how good you arc... There I have train more than 85 expert but your the brilliant one always wish you more success.

Regards,
Zarif

It's a more than complimentary email, but even reading it now brings me a sense of shame. I felt proud when I read it, but it also reminded me just how desperate for approval I was then, and still am. Actually, I should have known I did well on that course regardless. Yes, praise is always nice, but the evidence that I was capable should have been clear to me.

Every time I receive praise, I am aware of the flaw in my character that makes me need it. I'd grown up within systems where praise, given and received, was highly valued, and from day one I had enjoyed that process. Even my nursery had a programme of awarding stickers which you would collect on a piece of card, and the child with the most stickers at the end of term would win a book. I loved winning that book; my heart would nearly burst with excitement and I would fizz with pride. One year, when I was very young, I was so excited to go up on stage and collect my prize that I got up prematurely four times, waddling towards the stage with all the mothers hissing 'Not yet, not yet' at me!

All through my schooldays there was continual feedback on how you were doing. We were graded twice a term from when I started at boarding school at the age of ten, receiving marks in each subject for both Effort and Attainment. These marks were assimilated and then published in long lists that were posted on notice boards so you could figure out where you were ranked compared to your peers. At the end of every school year, the lists were used to calculate overall prizes. On leaving preparatory school at twelve I was awarded the Dux medal (an award given out in some Scottish schools to the pupil whose academic achievements are the highest in a school), and found myself every bit as excited as that toddler walking up to collect her prize. It was like that all through school, and then on to university, where, unless something was going to be graded, I didn't bother doing it. I had turned academic excellence into a performing art, and I needed the reviews to come in, glowing, with four or five stars attached.

I soon learned that this approach certainly didn't work

within an organisation like HALO and actually I don't think it does in many. I know there are performance reviews and other assessments, but these do not amount to the same thing. It is expected that, as an adult, you will be able to identify both your own good work and where to focus your attention. I was still so childlike in my craving of positive feedback, although I don't think it was merely egotistical (but I can't deny that it was to an extent). It was because I needed to know that I was doing the right thing. I am given to overthinking. I will always question myself, but far from bringing clarity, that will often fog my vision. Long after I finished university, I still craved guidance, whilst others are glad of the release into adulthood and the freedom to decide for themselves what is and isn't worthy.

Mozambique

Partly as a result of my performance on the course, I was assigned to a new project in Mozambique. It was late 2015, and the country had actually been declared landmine-free by this stage, but HALO still had a presence there, along with other international operators, to work on a UEMS task. UEMS stands for 'unplanned explosions at munitions sites', and this particular site was in Malhazine, a densely populated area of Mozambique's capital, Maputo. The Malhazine military munitions depot, originally built by the Portuguese colonial army, was the site of an accidental explosion in 2007, killing over 100 people and injuring some 500, following a previous explosion in 1985. The government wanted the site cleared not only because of the risk that the munitions housed there posed to residents, but also because it had plans to convert the site into a nature reserve.

We were working on munitions stored in the former Portuguese bunkers, while another demining organisation worked on the Mozambican military bunkers on the other side of the large site. Mozambique gained independence from Portugal in 1975. The bunkers were large concrete structures dug into the ground that housed everything from small-arms ammunition and grenades to mortar bombs and artillery shells. The day after I arrived in Maputo, I was taken to see them. The plan was centred on the need to establish time frames, but also safe procedures for disposing of items. The issue was that the site was located in the busy and populous capital. Moreover, the local residents were terrified. Many had either been there or had family members who had lived around the site at the time of the last explosion. They remembered the dreadful rumbles, the sounds of small and large explosions as different bunkers were affected, the munitions flying into people's homes. Understandably, the government had ordered that no items could be destroyed on-site, as it was likely that the sound of even these controlled demolitions would create panic among those living near by.

We drive along a busy street by the beachfront, the sea air blowing through the windows. It is very hot, but as usual, the old HALO vehicles don't have air-conditioning, and I was grateful for the cool, salty breeze, although I was already starting to sweat between the backs of my legs and the seat.

Misfire

We turn off into a maze of back alleys, driving for about fifteen minutes until we reached the former ammunition dump. The roads here aren't quite roads, they are red dusty tracks, but for the most part they are easy to handle in the HALO Land Rover. There is one point where the roots of a tree have created a series of humps and holes in the road and we slow down to drive over them. I make a mental note of the surroundings, so that I don't forget to slow for the dip when I drive to the site.

There are two sets of bunkers, one being cleared by HALO, the other by a different international operator. There is a gate at the entrance to the site, guarded by members of the Mozambican military, and just beyond that, a wide expanse of flat, sandy ground. To one side of it, is a small building, where other members of the military are sitting around on dusty, plastic chairs. We briefly stop there to view a collection of items that HALO has already found. Pits have been dug into this area to hold the unstable munitions, to minimise the damage from any accidental detonation.

The bunkers had been laid out in a circle, connected by a dirt track, which you could drive around, although usually we walked. It is actually a perfect layout for being able to oversee clearance in the various bunkers. We don't have enough teams to work in all the bunkers simultaneously, but actually this does mean we can spread the teams we do have around the circle so that if an accident were to take place, it wouldn't affect teams working on other bunkers. This is particularly important because we are using diggers and bulldozers to clear some of the bunkers. Each bunker

contained a different type of ammunition, and so each needs
to be assessed individually. An estimate is made of the volume
of the bunker and the dirt that needs to be combed through.
Some bunkers are far more badly damaged than others, but
what is clear on all is that ammunition was thrown outside
of the concrete bunkers when the explosion took place.
Therefore, the surrounding dirt, as well as any remains of
the bunker, must also be combed through to find the devices
that were launched into the surrounding area.

We have issues with Bunker 1, which was used to store
small-arms ammunition. This means there are literally
thousands of rounds each of which needs to be removed,
and it is taking far longer to clear than the original estimates.
We also have an issue with Bunker 2, where the team is
regularly encountering an item that we cannot identify. It's
tube-shaped, about 8/10 cm in length and perhaps 6 cm in
diameter. The ones we have found differ in their condition,
but many have sand lodged into an opening, either at
one or both ends. This is a problem, because if we don't
know what it is, we don't know how to handle or store it
safely. I carefully photograph it, and then e-mail the photos
around other HALO country programmes, asking if they
can identify it. One of the global staff comes out to give
us a hand, and he too is confused until we find out some
information that another organisation had previously tried
to perform some clearance on the site. It turns out that they
had found a load of white phosphorus grenades, and used
this bunker as the disposal site, piling them all in together
and trying to carry out a demolition, which clearly wasn't

successful. The demolition scattered the items within the ruins of the bunker and around the crater, where they have remained since, and now we are recovering them. Although some have sand lodged in both ends, others begin to smoke when they are uncovered.

This is a very serious problem for us. White phosphorus is an extremely nasty substance that burns on contact with air. If it makes contact with the skin, it will not stop burning – it will burn right through flesh to the bone, and then through the bone. During our medical training, we were shown photographs of white phosphorus burns, images that remain memorable for the horrendous injuries they depicted.

We immediately stop clearance at the white phosphorus bunker. We need to make a new plan. We also need to run a few practice casevac (casualty evacuation) exercises that focus on white-phos protocol, so that the teams are prepared should the worst happen. Additionally, we need masks for the teams while they are clearing, and to make sure they are all issued with gloves. We dig pits at a safe distance from the bunker, which can be used to smother any leaking grenades in wet soil, and buckets of water are placed on-site at all times.

This preparation only takes a few days, but that is valuable time that we can ill afford to spare. We are working to an exceptionally tight time frame, essentially because the time estimate that was made for the project was based on an out-of-date assessment. This proposal had been written before I arrived in the country, so I am having to work to this time frame, and as I begin to assess the situation it starts to look less and less possible. It is likely that we will have to ask for an extension, which the authorities will be unwilling to allow as they are keen to set about their plans for the nature reserve.

I'm based in the HALO house/office in Maputo, about a fifteen- to twenty-minute drive from the worksite. The clearance teams are staying on site, but I come back to the house/office each afternoon, once work has finished on the bunkers, in order to write up reports and work on the administrative side of running the site. We are using double-shifting on the site, which is when we have the manual clearance teams deploy in the morning for a full day's shift. Then there are two sets of mechanical teams, one group which deploys in the morning – they mainly use the diggers to spread out soil for the manual operators to sift through – and finishes just after lunchtime. The second set of mechanical teams works in the afternoon, doing a full day's work from lunchtime until early evening. The work in the afternoon is often digging into the craters, and partially destroyed bunkers, and creating heaps of soil and bunker debris that contain explosive items. These piles are then spread thinly by the diggers in the morning, so that the manual operators can carefully rake through them and find the items. Once the items have been removed, the cleared soil is collected by the digger and placed in a second heap, which will eventually be returned to the bunker. The double-shifting means we are far more efficient with this process, and it ensures that we are always prepared with plenty of soil and bunker debris for the manual teams to work through each morning.

Misfire

I wake up at just about 4 a.m. each morning, and make myself a cup of instant coffee. There is no milk so I have it black and very strong. I put in about half an inch of hot water to dissolve the dark dust at the bottom of my cup, and add half an inch of cold so that I can down it while I smoke a cigarette as I stand by my Land Rover in the dark. The drink is bitter and lukewarm, and exactly what I need to start the day. While making that coffee, I also put a large spoonful of instant coffee in a used plastic water bottle. I add some cold first so that the bottle doesn't melt, and then top it up with hot water from the kettle. I shake the bottle vigorously and tuck it in the side pocket of my backpack. I usually arrive at the work site at about 4:30 a.m., and spend the day supervising clearance, and assessing all the HALO bunkers to complete plans for clearance at each of them.

We have started to move the items of ammunition that have been found out to stores we have dug at the entrance to the worksite. These are deep pits at the entrance, to which we need to move the ammunition regularly as the shallow pits dug at each bunker are filling up quickly. Once the ammunition has been moved, I need to sort it carefully into each pit, and then each item is marked according to whether they are deemed safe to move or not – this is largely to do with whether there is still a fuse present, and whether, if the device was dropped or mishandled, it could still be initiated. Without a fuse, the device still contains the main explosive charge, but this explosive is far more stable, and so without the fuse it is very unlikely the device will function. We work out that the clearest way to mark them is with a dot of spray paint in either red (dangerous to move) or blue (safe to move). Actually, we will end up having to move all of it to a military central demolition site on the outskirts of Maputo. Normally, we would avoid transporting any potentially unsafe ammunition, but we aren't able to conduct any demolitions on site because the local people remember only too well the terrifying explosion of 2007.

I bought a couple of cans of paint at a local hardware store the day before, one red and one blue, so that I can start marking the ammunition that has already been moved, and check that it is placed into the correct pit. I begin by spraying a red dot on the unsafe ammunition, and then move on to marking with the blue paint. I squirt the first dot on to a mortar bomb. The wet paint shimmers in the sunshine, as fresh spray paint does. Except that, as the paint dries, it continues to shimmer. I take another look at the paint can, and realise that although the top is primary blue, the front proudly states 'metallic'. I am spray-painting decades-old ammunition with shimmery, metallic blue paint. I burst out laughing. I think of all the time and work I have put into being taken seriously, and now it looks like I have a penchant for sparkles. When I go back to the hardware store later to stock up on spray paint, it turns out that the only blue option is metallic, so on I go, trying to make the world a safer place, one glittery mortar bomb at a time!

Most days, I get back in the late afternoon/early evening, and then work on the bunker plans. This is a process of evaluating the information we have and working out solutions to various problems so that we can calculate new time estimates and submit a request for an extension to the Mozambican authorities. We also have to track the items found on a daily basis. On top of that, a big part of the reason why we are working on the site is to develop new standard operating procedures (SOPs) for safely clearing in and around buildings; for example, what we will do if we need to pull a wall down. This is because we are anticipating working in Syria at some point, which would mean conducting clearance in urban areas, so it was also partly a learning exercise (hence the huge amount of administrative work, documenting what was happening at the site).

Essentially, it's an admin-heavy task, which means there is lots to do each evening. There are a few problems with this routine, however. Firstly, I am not getting enough sleep, hence my insane addiction to bitter, lukewarm instant coffee. I have gone past exhaustion, and am now operating in a fatigued state as the norm. Secondly, I am not eating because of a clash of schedules. The teams based at the worksite have the budget for breakfast, lunch and dinner for the members of staff based there, but I am not included in that since I am not based in the camp at the site, but instead live in the HALO house that doubles as the office, and so I should be fed there.

By the time I get home in the afternoon I am extremely hungry, but as soon as I walk in the door my programme manager, who mainly works in the HALO house, wants to talk about the site. I then start in on the admin work, or head to the local hardware shop to pick up more supplies for the next day. I didn't speak to my parents much when I was in Mozambique – I simply didn't have time – but if I had explained what was going on, I already knew that my mother's advice would be, as always, that I needed to eat and sleep. To be honest, her words on that were already ringing in my ears without even speaking to her, and as sound as that advice is, I could hardly open a conversation about the food situation with 'My mum says...'!

The reason HALO provides food in their houses and offices across the world, is because much of the time you don't have the chance to look after yourself properly. It is part of what you are provided with as a HALO employee, to make sure you can get on with the work to the best of your ability. Most days I worked at least sixteen hours. I frequently mentioned this lack of food while I was working on the Malhazine project. It was understandable, in a way, because our work in Maputo was a completely different type of project from the traditional HALO mine-clearance programmes. The problem I think we all have is that there isn't the time to learn everything. I remember once asking my programme manager if there could please be something for me to eat when I got back, and his replying that he would ask for a 'nice salad', which in theory sounds lovely, but if you've already worked for twelve hours or more and are ravenously hungry, just isn't what you want to hear! I understood the reason: he was at meetings all day, but I was walking, carrying, lifting, and I needed something substantial to give me energy. I think there was a lack of understanding partly because we were at a strange phase in the project when everyone was working to different schedules, with different focuses, and that the point was missed that if I were to be based in the HALO house (as I was), there needed to be food for me there, since there wouldn't be any available for me at the site.

The situation improves significantly when the chief technical adviser joins us for a few weeks to oversee the changes on site, and to identify solutions to the difficult problems we are facing. But after he left things pretty much returned to normal. I smoke a lot, and I am losing weight quickly – over a stone in the space of a month. I feel tired and achy and my brain isn't as sharp as it was before. Eventually, things are resolved by my asking for the fridge to be filled with bread, cheese, ham and salad, and every morning as I make my inch of bitter coffee, I make a sandwich, wrap it in foil, and stuff it in my backpack. As I walk around in the sun, my lunch slowly warms and disintegrates but those soggy sandwiches are still the most delicious thing I have ever tasted.

Demolition

Just before Christmas, we complete our first bulk demolition. We need to get the ammunition out of busy central Maputo to the military central demolition site on the outskirts of the city. Much of the ammunition is marked with red spray paint as it would usually be categorised as unsafe to move. Unfortunately, we have no choice, so we have to find ways for us to move it with as little risk as possible. To reduce the danger to local residents we drive the ammunition out in the middle of the night, getting up at 2 a.m. to make our way to the sites and load the trucks. We have to be accompanied by a police escort, with one vehicle at the front of the convoy, and one at the back. We have one big truck, carrying the unsafe to move ammunition, I drive the vehicle behind that, and I think following me is the programme manager's car carrying him and the global technical expert: his position is a roaming one, and he travels to any HALO programme that needs additional technical assistance. He's here because of the complexity of the project; it is very different to straightforward mine clearance and we need additional support. He is also here because, as mentioned before, there is a hope that the lessons learned on this site may be helpful to future clearance in more urbanised areas than HALO currently works in. We are also joined by members of the Mozambican military, including a general.

We had set up three pits of ammunition for the bulk demolition. We have one of the teams with us, and together they dig three pits as well as a small dugout 300 metres away to be used as the firing point. The global technical adviser, the programme manager, and I then carefully stack each pit with ammunition. We run the firing cables that will carry the electric charge to the detonators back to the firing point 300 metres away. The shells in the top layer are primed with explosives, before detonators are placed, and then the upper part of each pit is backfilled with soil.

While the charges were being placed, the team that had accompanied us to dig the pits and unload the ammunition move back along the roads that provide access to the demolition site, blocking them to secure the 1,500-metre safety distance around the pits. This is known as a cordon, and it makes sure no one walks or drives into the site during the demolition. The points where the team are placed on these roads are agreed beforehand by creating a circle on a map that gives you a distance of 1.5 kilometres from the pits. Grid references of the points where this circle meets any roads, or where there are any other points you would like to place someone are taken, and then given to the teams, who use their GPS devices to travel to the correct points where they remain as sentries. The final access route is blocked by the programme manager and global technical adviser, and once they are in place, I move to the firing point, 300 metres from the pits. It is a small dugout cut into the back of a termite mound and padded with sandbags filled from hours of laborious digging in the sun-baked soil. I radio the team to complete a cordon check, ensuring the perimeter is secure, and on that being confirmed I say 'Quiet, firing' into my radio as I turn the firing key of the Beethoven (a Beethoven exploder is a hand-cranked device used to fire electrical detonators) to fire the first pit. The firing key is slotted into a corresponding hole in the side of the Beethoven, and then you hold in a button at the same time as rotating the key faster and faster until you hear the explosion. There is a rule that whoever is going to be doing the firing keeps the firing key with them at all times, so no one can accidentally set off the charge while someone is still present at the demolition site. The sound of the explosion washes over me and shrapnel begins to whiz overhead and land around me, and I sit in my sandbag den waiting for the dust to settle before setting off the second pit and another successful demolition.

In the final pit, we were trialling a new firing device to initiate the detonators, one that sent a signal to a receiving device located next to the pit. Having gone through the usual radio procedures, I flick off the safety catch and press the button – unlike the Beethoven there is no firing key to turn. Nothing happens. I wait and press again. Still nothing. At this point I use my radio to call a misfire and notify the cordon, and then I begin to walk back to the pit to see what has happened. I remember that walk back so clearly. You go forward alone; it's known in the mine clearance sector as 'one man one risk'.

I have always tried to keep superstition out of my mind when working, because believing that inanimate objects have feelings and intentions can render you pretty useless when you're dealing with explosive devices. But this time I have a bad feeling. A really bad feeling. The fact of the matter is that we have never used a firing device like this until now; we were only using it to ignite thermite charges to destroy white phosphorus grenades at the city centre site. Thermite is a pyrotechnic composition, rather than an explosive. It is used to burn the white phosphorus grenades and causes no explosion, meaning that it could be used at the city site without alarming the (justifiably) nervous locals. Here we were on a military central demolition site, already littered with ammunition from previous demolitions that have not been cleared properly. Walking back towards the pit is deeply unsettling – if the main charges go up at that distance there is little that will protect me.

I am momentarily afraid, but then my mind seems to take over. It just kept running over procedures: had I put the safety catch back on the firing device, did I have the firing key from the Beethoven in my top pocket, did I have my insulation tape, was my knife in there too? I have this fleeting feeling of fear, and then complete calm. The only other time I can remember that happening was when I was in the car crash as a teenager. When we went over the edge into a steep valley it was the same blinding flash of fear as I realised what was happening, and then I can remember being almost icily calm as I heard the driver scream on the way down. It's one of my clearest memories – as though that flash of pure fear opens a door to another level of thinking.

I remember everything from resetting that third pit. I had decided at that point not to continue with the radio firing device we were trialling, and revert instead to the traditional method of using the Beethoven, as this had worked successfully for the first two pits. So, I move the firing cable that had been blown out of the first pit, and connect it to the detonator in the third pit. I remember trying to move that cable over quickly and efficiently, and not let it get caught in the small, dry shrubs. Trimming the black and brown insulation from the end of the wires. Connecting the detonator. Turning my back on the pit and walking to the firing point. Checking the cordon over the radio. Putting the firing key into the Beethoven (the same one used successfully to fire the first two pits) and beginning to turn. I sit in my sandbagged shelter until the shrapnel stops flying and the dust settles. Job done.

The second drill went absolutely fine, but it brought an interesting reframing of my understanding of fear and where it sits in our consciousness. Over the years I had consistently spoken about how I wasn't scared when I was doing my job, and that I knew exactly what I was doing. That doesn't really account for how you will react in an unusual situation, one for which you are unprepared, and to be honest that is very much like life itself. We forget, sometimes, how much of what we do is instinctive, how it is built into our very biology and reinforced by the nurturing we receive when we are young, and I believe that you have to give yourself a break for the things you feel that are involuntary. For flashes of rage and jealousy, for moments of abject fear. In fact, there is a great deal to learn from them, as indicated by the sheer amount we talk about 'gut instinct'.

An appreciation of the way your body instinctively tries to protect you from pain, or to warn you of danger is hugely important to informed decision-making, but it is also important to remember that it doesn't know the full story. Being able to entertain those biological reactions, to assess their meaning, is one thing, but these must be put into context of the situation. For example, on that day I knew exactly the right thing to do, I knew I could regain control of the situation. I knew that the difference between its going right or wrong ultimately lay with me. My body's reaction to the situation was entirely instinctive; but what it didn't know is that I had both the skills and the tools to resolve the situation. So yes, you can manage fear, although that doesn't mean stepping blindly into the unknown. It's about knowing yourself, your abilities and your boundaries – and working out whether it's the moment to take a deep breath, steady yourself, and step forward, or whether it is smarter (and sometimes even braver) to take a step back. I didn't know it then, but this was something that I would remember in the coming weeks.

Shortly after the demolition, it was time for the Christmas break, when I was taking two weeks leave. HALO held a large staff meeting (known as the Annual Cross-Briefing) over three days at Drumlanrig Castle, near to the HQ in Thornhill, and then I went home to spend Christmas with my family. Over Christmas, my mum, younger sister and I went shopping with my older sister for her wedding dress. We went to a local shop in Dumfries, but to be honest, she was never going to get her dress from this shop. It wasn't her thing at all, but I think she wanted to give me a chance to feel involved. The ordinariness of it all was a familiarity that I thought I craved, but I couldn't connect with any of what was going on. I felt as though I was going through the motions, that I was 'acting normal'. I almost felt that I was outside my body watching myself trying to say and do the right things, but that inside I was numb to it all.

Then, over New Year, I attended a friend's wedding in England with all the gang from university. I've never been the most sociable of people, but on this occasion I really struggled. I didn't know what to say about the past couple of months, how to explain what I had been doing. Worse, I wasn't really sure what questions to ask my friends. I spent my whole time with them terrified of putting my foot in it, of asking about something that had already happened or talking about someone they didn't want to talk about. I felt completely out of touch. I was sharing a room with Bessie, an old friend from university, and I couldn't sleep the first night. I tossed and turned, not managing a wink of sleep. After the wedding, I woke up screaming in the middle of the night, which Bessie still recalls vividly.

On 4 January 2016, I flew back to Mozambique, after a brief stop in Scotland to pick up my work clothes. I unpacked my wedding outfit from a suitcase, and repacked my HALO clothes into my bag, then took the flight to London, on from there to Johannesburg, finally arriving in Maputo the next day. I walked back into my room in Mozambique and felt my spirits sink. I didn't belong here. I didn't belong there, at home. I didn't belong anywhere any more.

The work began again, this time without the help of the global technical expert. It was as punishing and as time-consuming as before, but now it felt like the responsibility for everything running safely and efficiently at the site lay firmly on my shoulders. I felt unsupported, and similar problems with the food situation recurred. Walking around the site one day, I find the white phosphorus grenades are being rinsed in a bucket of water, without gloves or face protection being used, and while the teams are working on site. It is a calculated risk, but I'm surprised I have not been told first. I would be happy for us to go through a process of trying to work out which of the items we are storing actually contain any white phosphorus, but I believe that this should be done without the teams there to minimise risk to anyone else, and with the correct protective gear. Quite apart from anything else, it sets a poor example to the teams on site, especially as we have been telling them to take particular care when working in this bunker. Many of the grenades proved to be empty, and were simply stuffed with sand all the way through, but this new approach seems at odds with everything we have discussed and planned to minimise any risks at this bunker over the preceding weeks.

Something inside me snaps. I have put so much time and effort into this project. I haven't eaten or slept properly in weeks. I think the main thing I felt was that I should have been told first, so that I knew what was happening that day, rather than me coming around the corner to find it happening without my knowledge. I think we would collectively acknowledge how tricky the whole Malhazine task has been, but this just felt like a kick in the face, and undermined my position on the site, as well as all the work I had put in.

In the days that followed, or it may even have been the same day, I rang my country director from the worksite and handed in my notice. I remember pacing in the sand at the medical point while on the phone to him, sweating, guilt twisting my gut but I just knew I shouldn't be there any more. I felt I wasn't working within a framework I could understand, and that I was without guidance or allies. I have never felt more alone.

What probably affected me as deeply, I think, was that

it is was very hard to see the humanitarian imperative for the project. Certainly, it is not ideal to have a site covered in unexploded ammunition that has been subject to heat and pressure in the middle of town, but unless the land was being used the risk was minimal. Regenerating land for a nature reserve doesn't really fall under the humanitarian imperative. It certainly wasn't the same as other projects, where people are desperate to reclaim the land you are clearing, and where it is essential in order to allow them to live safely.

I will come on to my final remaining months with HALO in Zimbabwe, for there were experiences there that are worth recording, I think. Before that, I'd like to acknowledge that I took this situation, and the resulting sensation of being undermined and deserted, very personally. With hindsight, it was resolvable. But I should also say that, as much as I feel disappointed at myself, as much as I look back and want to scream 'You're hungry, and exhausted, but you can discuss this with the people involved and resolve it,' I do think the decision to leave was likely the correct choice to make at the time.

Friends still at HALO now tell me there have been big changes in the years since I left. There are more women than ever working for them now, and while it is still hard work in dangerous places, the macho culture is a thing of the past.

I was very proud to work for HALO, and that was part of the reason that my decision to leave was so difficult. I can't deny that I still carry a lot of guilt and shame about it. Perhaps I have never really allowed myself to process those emotions properly, but a part of me is also very glad I handed in my notice at that point. Over the course of those few months at Malhazine I had lost so much weight that it was starting to become a problem. I managed to put a bit back on in Zimbabwe, but really, I needed to get back to feeling healthy, partly because of a lack of stamina, but also because poor health affects the way your brain functions. I was walking around in a daze. I wasn't eating and sleeping properly, and so was smoking forty a day and drinking bitter lukewarm coffee from an old plastic bottle just to get by. Even emotionally, I had forgotten how to laugh, as though I had no personality, as though my body couldn't summon the energy to feel enthused about anything. I used to be curious, excitable, and angry. I burned with rage and excitement. But the fire had gone out, completely.

It felt like I had been smothered and stifled and that I needed to breathe again. It was a feeling I hated, but sometimes the right thing to do is to walk away. It felt uncomfortable. It was not the plan. There are levels of heartbreak, and not all of them spring from romantic love. Realising that it is time to step away from something can be equally gut-wrenching, and it can still make you question whether you are worthy. I hadn't really walked away from anything before, but I suddenly had a better understanding of the people I knew who decided to leave university, or change courses, or give up jobs that everyone else told them they were lucky to have, or end relationships that others thought were perfect, or take time out of friendships that seemed enduring. I remembered not really understanding their decisions at the time, and how most people questioned them. Now I felt bad for not having been able to identify with their choices before.

True, you have control, in a way, because you have made the decision. But that doesn't make it less heartbreaking. In a way, it makes you question it more, because it was your choice and you've laid everything on the line for it. You feel that if things turn out badly, the blame will be laid firmly at your door. This, I think, is why life decisions can be so hard. It is often easy to work out what is wrong for you, but nowhere near as easy to find what is right. As a result, you can end up in what feels like a pattern of bad decisions. Actually, each is just teaching you a little about what is wrong, to try to set you on the right path. One problem with that, however, is the perceptions of those around you, which can make you feel that you're floundering. I think that this is why your mid-twenties can often just feel like a series of bad decisions, because you don't realise that you are cutting your teeth for the rest that life brings.

I remain conflicted about this time, even though everything ultimately turned out for the best. By the same token, however, I can never know that things wouldn't have panned out better had I stayed. I can argue both sides of the case, and even now I still do. But just as there is never any point in wondering what life would have been had you not broken up with someone, so too I should not have dwelt on that decision in the way I did. I had made it, and I needed to move on. So, one thing I did learn from this experience, is that you have to allow yourself closure. It's only fair. Hard decisions are hard precisely because they have no obvious answer.

Zimbabwe

I was due to hand over the project in Mozambique at the end of January 2016, and to return to Zimbabwe as programme officer, which combines some aspects of the technical field officer position, alongside some of the projects officer skills, such as report writing and NGO partnerships. When I arrived there, things felt immediately better. I did start to gain a bit of weight, although I was still busy so it wasn't exactly piling on. I also worked on a couple of extremely interesting projects. One of them was aimed at developing MRE (mine-risk education) material for children with a local charity that produced books, the other involved my calculating the use of electricity in the camp. We were still using a 5kVA generator to run the camp, but were looking to change to solar power and had to come up with an estimate of how many panels, converters and batteries we would need. We were also working towards a large donor visit from DFID (Department for International Development), shortly before I was due to depart the country.

There are two operations managers in Zimbabwe, one an Eritrean expatriate and the other a Zimbabwean, and I joined them one day to see the work they were doing to train new demining staff, having secured more funding to increase the number of teams. The three of us were in the training camp early one morning, when it began to rain heavily. Thunder echoed in the distance, and lightning flashed across the sky. My first thought was 'Oh no'. The last time we had a storm like this, it had been at night and several of the tents had been torn to pieces. We had all run around the camp in the rain and the dark, trying to secure the canvas as it flapped in the wind. On the following morning, we had to pause clearance to allow the kit to dry. The last thing we needed, I thought, before a big donor visit, was for the camp to be partially destroyed. As it turns out that could not have been further from the last thing we wanted.

A panicked call comes in over the radio. It was still early morning, and work only began a couple of hours before. There has been an accident. At this point we are confused. When it rains the deminers shelter under the tarpaulin at the medical point – you can't work in the rain as the water runs down the visor and you can't see properly. We had heard the call for demining to cease come through about five or ten minutes earlier, so how could there have been an accident? The voice on the radio is screaming and fearful. We jump in the vehicle and head straight there. One of the operations managers takes a call, but he can't understand the person at the other end, and so he passes the phone to me. Meanwhile the other operations manager focuses on the radio. It's a confused message, but there are a few things we can make out '…lightning, lightning…he's dead.'

We arrive to a devastating scene. The team had been standing, as they should have been, under the tarpaulin at the medical point when they were hit directly by a bolt of lightning. Five of them are injured, and two more were rendered immediately unconscious, their hearts stopped by the electric shock. The head medic has managed to revive one of these men, but the other is dead. He is loaded into our vehicle and covered with a sheet, to be driven to the nearest hospital so that the official paperwork can be completed. The other victims are also rushed to the hospital to be treated.

On the drive back to camp with the Zimbabwean manager, he tells me a story. He says that this minefield was meant to have been cleared maybe ten years ago, when a commercial demining organisation was carrying out the work. It was earmarked as important for linking the local village with the border. They began clearance but there was a terrible accident, and then some of the local people came and told them that they should not be disturbing this land. They were superstitious about it and said strange things happen there sometimes, things they could not explain. So the commercial staff stopped work in that area and left it uncleared. There is a large baobab tree there, which the locals believe is cursed. An accident on that same minefield, during HALO clearance, resulted in one of our team losing his finger. Some locals believe this was a warning. In fact, minor accidents like that aren't all that uncommon. They aren't an everyday occurrence, of course, but they have happened all along this stretch of clearance. It is only this accident that makes people think now that it was a warning for us to have stopped.

In truth, though, the accident was completely unexpected – the demining team weren't even sheltering under the biggest tree in the area. It was one of those awful, random things that happens, which no one can explain. Later that day, we go to tell the man's widow. Lots of the staff are from this village and we don't want the news to come to her another way. It turns out that she has heard there had been an accident, she just didn't know who was involved. She is standing outside her house as our vehicle pulls up and you can see it written all over her face – 'Please don't tell me what I think you're going to tell me. Please, *please* don't.' As the operations manager opens his mouth to speak, her face falls. She just knows. She crumples to the ground and begins to sob, her shoulders hunched forward. Her two children toddle over, confused about what is wrong, and she tries to hold them as they become increasingly upset by her anguished sobs. We are all crouching in a wide circle around her. The women in the surrounding houses start to come out and make their way over to her. Holding her, slowly forming a protective wall around her. Sobbing alongside her. Her life as a widow will be difficult, her children's lives are irreparably changed, their chances of success suddenly drastically lowered. HALO organises the funeral with the family, providing food and shelter for the mourners. As is customary, work ceases until the body has been buried, but we still have the big donor visit, and so the programme manager, operations manager and I host them in the camp, and show them through the now quiet, partially cleared minefields, while the rest of the staff remain stood down to mourn.

The day of the funeral was like watching the trial of an innocent person. Watching as a life is ripped apart, endlessly punished for crimes they did not commit. Watching them suffer. I feel like a spectator watching from the balcony, as though I could stand up and scream and nothing would happen, nothing would change. You want to take away the other person's pain, you want to put yourself in their shoes. And yet, at the most basic human level, you are relieved that it is not you, that your family live in relative safety. That's the worst thing of all, because where do you put this wretched feeling, this selfish, self-preserving feeling? How do you ever forgive that dark part of yourself that is grateful it isn't you?

I couldn't. It is unforgivable.

Chapter 5

Guilt

———

It was only a few weeks later, late in the spring of 2016, that I was due to finish my time with HALO and return home. When I got back, I suffered badly from OCD tendencies. I've always had these since I was very young. I used to have about twenty stuffed animals that I kept in a small hammock, strung up above my childhood bed. Every night, I would be given a small plastic beaker of warm milk to help me sleep, and every night, I would carefully feed each of the animals the exact same amount of warm milk by tipping the beaker to their mouths. I would worry if I had accidently tipped too much into one, thinking the others would be upset, and so I would start all over again, trying to make sure they had exactly equal amounts. Aside from the fact that they began to smell awfully of rotten milk – which, as everyone knows, is vile – the level of stress this caused me before going to bed was ridiculous. I would worry and worry about it. If I had finished 'feeding' each of them, and turned my light off but then had a funny feeling, I would turn my light on and start the whole process again, because I was convinced that otherwise something terrible would happen.

I taught myself such unhealthy patterns of control. I did a lot of tapping door handles, locking and unlocking doors multiple times, standing on the 'right' cracks in the pavement, and I wore the same clothes over and over again if something had gone well on the day when I first wore them. I was always trying to mask these things, particularly when I went away to boarding school. I would pretend I had forgotten something so I could tap a door handle again, as if I was going back into the room to check whether the forgotten item was there. When I walked along the paths between school buildings, I would pretend that I was trying to avoid things so that I could stand exactly on the right lines in the paving. I grew out of this, to an extent, although even now, any time when I am under particular stress, I will revert to these techniques to try to calm myself, because it makes me feel that I can control uncontrollable situations.

I spent a few weeks in Scotland before I moved down to London to be near my friends. I actually found being at home very difficult at that time, as I had too much going on in my head, and I wasn't ready to answer questions. I also truly didn't know what was going to happen next in my life. So I didn't want to talk about the past, and I didn't want to talk about the future, and on a day-to-day basis, I didn't really have much going on. My parents are lovely people, and they like to chat and engage with their children, and I knew that I wasn't in the right frame of mind to do so. I moved to London as quickly as I could, into a small downstairs room in a house with three of my friends. They had lived there since leaving university, with different members of our circle of friends moving in and out. I managed to find an interesting job in cyber security, working for a small team with two brilliant bosses, and I was initially relatively happy.

Except, I definitely wasn't. I was mixed up, which I found unbearable. I now realise that this was from a combination of a conflicted sense of self, and likely PTSD. I found that I couldn't deal with the frustration I felt at such an unfair world, in which I could do so little to change things. I feel guilt very keenly, and that period of time I remember viscerally. If I even think about it, I feel a tightening in my chest. I hated myself even more for that sense of guilt, because I was able to dip in and out of opposing worlds, whereas the people I had left behind had no such luxury. I had no right to be back in the UK, trying to establish some sort of a social life. I felt selfish, and I hated that quality in myself and berated myself for it every day. I could not stop thinking about the just-widowed mother and her two children, and then those thoughts would spiral into memories of others I had met, who had similarly been dealt cruel injustices through no fault of their own.

When I reflect now, I think there were a number of things going on, but at the time, I couldn't untie the threads to work out what was causing the knot tightening in my chest. I never worked to unravel this at that time. To HALO's credit, I was offered therapy after the accident in Zimbabwe.

But I didn't take them up on the offer, for two reasons. Firstly, it felt so wrong to have absorbed that secondary trauma and considered it to be a legitimate reason to ask for support. What had happened wasn't about me, and I didn't feel justified in seeking help. Secondly, I had had no good experiences of therapy. When I first went away to boarding school I suffered bad panic attacks, and the sanatorium at school brought a specialist in to speak to me, and I found the whole process extremely difficult. I think that for many others it would have been a different experience, a helpful one that brought them a sense of relief. But for me, it felt like a reinforcement of my own suspicions that I was a bit odd, while I also struggled with talking about emotion. In therapy, I felt under pressure to produce the right answers, and in consequence I think I often just said what I thought the therapist wanted to hear, as I was used to doing with the teachers in class.

For me, therapy did not seem like a safe space where I could explore the way I was feeling. It felt like a pressure cooker, into which everything that I had managed to keep separate and tidied away would all be thrown together and brought to boiling point. I didn't feel that I could handle it. Even now, the thought of sitting in a room and talking about myself sends me close to a panic attack. I have tried numerous approaches and never made it beyond six sessions of any kind. I tried CBT, but the person I was speaking to had no understanding of the context of my work, and trying to explain all the nuances and complexities was so difficult that I would end up frustrated and overwhelmed. To this day,

Guilt

I have never successfully discussed the things that I remain hung up on from my time working abroad.

The truth is that I'm not entirely sure whether or not I suffered from PTSD. What kept happening, I think, was that when I read about it my initial thoughts were immediately, *I could not and should not be the one with PTSD just because I had been witness to traumatic or disturbing events, rather than the victim of them.* I was unable to understand how secondary trauma could cause me to feel this way, although in my heart of hearts I knew how troubled I was by having been a bystander to others' pain. There are times from childhood when I remember my brother or one of my sisters being upset, and thinking about it now troubles me far more than any memories of my own pain. I literally can't bear it. So maybe I hadn't adequately dealt with the many distressing things I had seen during my time with HALO, both through the work but also from residing in places where people's lives often involved dreadful hardship. Perhaps because of my guilt at feeling upset by this, however, I tried to process this information without its seeming as though it was affecting me in any way at all.

The symptoms that something just wasn't right were perhaps most telling. I felt irritable most of the time. I struggled to sleep properly; my brain was always slightly more awake than it needed to be. When I was younger, I slept very heavily, but now the lightest of noises would wake me, and it would feel like that moment when someone jumps out from behind a door. I would get this sudden huge rush of adrenaline, leaving me feeling wide awake and alert. I also constantly felt isolated. I actually love my own company;

I'm introverted by nature and enjoy spending time alone, so I have often struggled to explain what I mean by feeling isolated, since most people who know me recognise that I enjoy being on my own.

The isolation was a completely different feeling to that which I had experienced when I felt lonely working abroad, because it was a sense of being alone despite being surrounded by people. I often felt as though I knew something other people didn't. I hated travelling on the underground because I felt so uneasy, like something was going to happen. I struggled badly with choosing things to buy in the supermarket. I would go in and feel so confused. I couldn't remember having this much choice and I didn't know how to go about selecting what I wanted. For the most part, you are fed while you are with HALO, and I had completely forgotten how to plan what to eat.

The OCD tendencies also struck me worst when I had to make day-to-day decisions like buying food. I kept thinking, that if I made the wrong decision something bad would happen. I would touch each of the cans of baked beans to try to work out which one was the 'lucky one'. Choosing an apple became a stressful process, for if I picked one up and it felt wrong, I had to exchange it. This habit became so ingrained at this time that I am still unable to avoid it when I go into a shop by myself. I can only really shop successfully in a supermarket if I am with someone who I know will keep me in check. This doesn't mean that they know of my tendency, but is because I will be too embarrassed to go through the whole process in front of them, since they would notice it. I still mainly shop online because it takes the stress out of the situation for me.

During moments of extreme stress the brain is flooded with cortisol and adrenaline. This is partly to ensure that the moment is committed to memory, to avoid getting into the same situation again. It is one of our evolutionary protective processes.

I began to realise that certain situations would unlock these memories, particularly walking through brightly lit supermarkets, or anywhere that had cool fluorescent lighting. I still have no idea why this should trigger those thoughts to reappear. I am a wildly sentimental person, and I had usually managed bad memories from the past by not listening to the songs that reminded me of them, or not watching the TV shows that would make me think about things I didn't want to think about. However, fluorescent lighting is surprisingly hard to avoid, and the memories just kept spilling out of the box in which I had tried to tuck them away.

I also found silence very difficult, so whenever I could, I would listen to YouTube videos, audiobooks or podcasts, but of course that wasn't always possible at work. The office I worked in was a lovely working environment in terms of people, but the lighting, alongside many hours inside my own head because of the silence in the office, meant that I found I was suffering an overwhelming number of distressing thoughts. At this point, another defence mechanism took over – dissociation. In trying to avoid the emotional pain and stress, my brain sought to protect me by slowly numbing me. This was when I started to become badly confused. I definitely didn't piece it all together like that. Instead, to me it felt as though my life had no meaning any more, and I decided I needed to go back to working in something in which I would feel fulfilment.

I missed having physical tasks to complete, which I found immensely satisfying and the best way to keep my mind focused, and not dwelling on events of the past. I was very lucky to be offered a position in Afghanistan with another charity, the Danish Demining Group, and decided to take it. I handed in my one-month's notice, about which my bosses were exceptionally kind, and on the day I left, everyone from the office went across the road to the pub for drinks. They gave me a basket of British snacks to take with me, and a small flip knife with my name engraved on the handle. It was one of the most thoughtful gifts I had ever been given. I should add here that the kindness shown me through the months I worked at this company is something I often think about. Everyone was supportive of each other, contributing to a very equal environment, and in other circumstances I believe I would have thrived there.

It is worth noting that this was still a sector (STEM) where women were massively underrepresented. When I joined the company (which was then a very small start-up) I was the only woman, but I never really felt like this was a factor. The feedback was clear as well: I was praised when something went right, and given assistance when I couldn't complete something. I do think it is worth noting this, just as much as it is worth noting when things felt like they had gone the other way. Firstly, to give credit where it is due. But secondly, because there are always so many questions about how were we to do things right, and so I try to understand why an environment felt different, and why and how it affected the people within it. In this case, I think it was because everyone looked at each other, regardless of position or gender, as if they had something valuable to contribute to the team, and took into account that different people have different skills. It was the way people spoke to each other as people, both in terms of work and outside of it. There were genuine questions about people's lives, as well as a genuine and respectful interest in each person's role within the organisation.

The crux of it was that the company avoided becoming a competitive environment. No one had to beat someone else down for their work to be seen and respected. There were a lot of meetings where any difficulties faced by different team members were discussed and learned from, but it wasn't an environment in which people were exposed or berated. Being without that fear or friction was instrumental in my learning that you do not need them in order to have progress. It was a lesson worth learning, not just for the workplace, but also more generally within an increasingly antagonistic social media world.

This may sound pretty unobservant of me, but up until that point, I hadn't realised that in every other place where I had worked I had felt that I was pitted against someone else. Sometimes, I think people often believe that if you are someone who likes to do what you do well, you will thrive in a competitive environment. I am not actually sure that is the case, however, because you need to have rock-solid belief in yourself to accomplish that and that is very rare. To be honest, I sometimes think that people misinterpret self-belief into the idea that everything they do is 100 per cent right, 100 per cent of the time, and I think that is an incredibly dangerous notion. It should not be considered a weakness to be consistently re-evaluating your skills and your work in an attempt to improve them.

I am diffident to the point of it being an annoyance, both to others and myself. However, I would also hate to live with a steadfast belief that I am always right. At school and university I was invariably the person who came out of exams convinced that I had failed. This frustrated my friends at the time, because often I would have done very well, but much later in life I spoke to someone about the habit, and she gave me probably one of the most useful pieces of information I have ever received. My brain likes to solve problems; in fact it actively looks for them. When I came out of an exam, the first thing I would do is fixate on the question that I had suddenly realised I had got wrong. I would not be able to get it out my head because it would be stuck in a loop, something like: I got that question wrong, I would like to correct it, I can't correct it because the exam has finished and I have missed the opportunity to get it right, I got that question wrong, I can't correct it because the exam has finished and I have missed the opportunity to get it right...

It was those situations, where I couldn't change what had been, or perhaps it was something that I could not change at all, that wound the tension in my brain to its highest point. It didn't just apply in an academic sense, either. Imagine seeing a picture of a young woman with long legs in the context that that is the ideal figure to have, and then looking at your own legs, and realising they are quite short as you are only 5 foot 3 inches tall, and then your brain clocks that it cannot change that, but wait, you need to be attractive, but it's not physically possible. Here is another endless loop. Does this sound familiar – obsessing over things you cannot change? As a state of mind, it is such a double-edged sword. A part of it means that you will do everything in your power to get whatever it is right the first time, because you know you will not be able to handle a negative outcome if you could have avoided it. It will make you hard-working and conscientious. Sometimes, another part of it will mean that you plan for things others don't, which can be exceptionally frustrating, especially if they cannot see it from your viewpoint. Often, you will have a helicopter view of situations, and be able to see several possible outcomes, whereas others may only see the first immediate problem, and try to solve that without necessarily thinking of the future consequences of such an action and whether, in reality, it will actually create further issues to solve. The worst part of all of it is that you will dwell on any mistakes, however well-intentioned, and while this will help you learn, it will also often leave you afraid to make another one.

To be honest, I think highly competitive working environments are often counterproductive, in that they do not account for more introspective and self-effacing characters to thrive, despite the very real benefits such individuals can offer. To me, if you are already beating yourself up for what you got wrong, you rarely, if ever, need someone else to join in and kick you when you are down. You need someone to help you find the thing you missed, to help you learn from the experience, not to send you running in fear of it. Bearing in mind that I am not a psychiatrist, I found this a very helpful explanation of why I will on occasion become caught up in something, because my brain keeps trying to find a way to go back and resolve it. But I also know that is why when, in anyone else's eyes *everything* was going well for me, I would be caught up in the memories of the things I could not change.

The worst, and most prevailing, feeling was guilt. Sickening guilt. For me, the predominant solution I found to avoid feeling that guilt, was alcohol. This was perhaps even more alluring for me because it also took the edge off the OCD. If I could get myself to the level of being slightly dizzy drunk, I stopped worrying about flicking lights on and off or touching door handles. That release was something I craved desperately from day to day. The thing is, I didn't realise how dangerous it was for me to be drinking like that. In moderation, fun nights and alcohol are an escape, and as far back as history remembers, it has been shown that people need some kind of release to balance their lives. Drugs, sex and alcohol (perhaps even love) are often presented as solely evil, but they are not really. They are a normal part of life, when motivated by normal emotions, and handled with a healthy respect. What was far more dark and sinister, was the fact that I could not find a different solution to my negative emotions.

Guilt

This guilt led me to examine how I felt about the work I had done or had seen being carried out, and I couldn't shake this feeling of being tainted by white saviourism. There were moments that would return to my mind over and over again. I remembered once in Cambodia seeing a toddler standing outside his home in a distinctly impoverished border town. The child was naked from the waist down, although it wasn't all that uncommon there to see children who didn't have full sets of clothing. The child, a boy, was facing away from me, and as I scanned the area with my eyes, taking in the scene, he defecated in a huge molten pile. He actually barely seemed to notice that he was doing it. I realised that there was a mass of small white worms squirming around in the stomach-churning mound he had deposited on the ground. Moments later, the child came running towards me, reaching out his fingers, holding up his sweet little chubby arms, demanding to be picked up and played with. His face was lit by an enormous smile. His mother did not know what to do; there was no local health clinic, and the family were desperately poor. But I also did not know what to do. How could I? I did not have a child of my own, I was not a medical professional, and yet in that moment I could see the people around me looking for answers and decisions that I was not equipped to make. It would have been easy for me in those circumstances to offer advice, and maybe I might even have felt better if I had provided some, even if it might not have been correct. Maybe then I would have felt that I was helping.

It was the hardest thing to do, not to pick up that

poor child and hold him. And yet what if I had gone on to another village after that, and another healthy child ran up to hold my hand, and I passed something on to another family without access to a health clinic? It was hard not to sit with the mother and advise her on how to keep her home clean. I did not have any experience of living in her home, or trying to keep a child clean and food untainted in those conditions. I didn't even have a common language with them to ensure they would fully understand any advice I could give. As uncomfortable as it was to admit it, it simply wasn't my place to float into their desperate situation, and offer potentially damaging advice or behaviour. This was not my area of experience or expertise, but it is odd how you feel obligated to offer assistance in such situations. Yet I wonder how well we are able to help or offer advice on both an individual and a collective level. When someone is struggling, we often look to offer an opinion, and I think that can be in part due to it making us feel like we have done something. Of course, sometimes we may have something constructive to offer, but on other occasions I think it can be more to do with our feelings and with allowing us to step away from the situation with a sense of self-congratulation about what we have contributed. However, frequently people are looking for support, acknowledgement of their struggles, and an ongoing engagement with their needs, rather than an opinion (that could be ill-informed). I try to remember that now, not just in work but in friendships, too.

I spent a lot of those months in London dwelling on the past. I couldn't quite figure out where the lines of good and bad fell, where I had let people down, or where I had been let down. Good intentions are simply not good enough. That sounds extreme, but it is possible to do a great deal of harm with the best of intentions. I was extremely privileged in many of the places I went to. The protection and entitlement I had experienced in my life, simply on the basis of being born in a particular place, into comfortable economic and social circumstances, or looking a particular way, was always evident.

Racism is institutionalised, and we cannot avoid how the power structures in the world have created the environment for the systemic marginalisation of people. Although this is not a like-for-like comparison, sexism is similarly systemic and institutionalised by power structures, and I was also aware of the gender disparity that existed within these structures. You can have experienced discrimination, and also be a perpetrator, and we need to get better at recognising that. It is deeply uncomfortable to confront the fact that you yourself may have been complicit in perpetuating ideas and systems that were built on the basis of unfounded beliefs of superiority. But it is important we do, for 'white saviourism' is not only not the answer, it is degrading and deeply damaging. Equally, understanding where discrimination intersects is vital to the realisation of effective and sustained change.

Often, the problem stems from the most privileged shaping our view of the world, and choosing what to show and what to conceal. Thus, what we are permitted to see fits with their narrative, and indeed this can go further in terms of being a calculated act to serve their agenda. It is the reason our Western view of the world is so overwhelmingly white and male, despite all evidence to the contrary. That version of the world has become their accepted truth. Repeatedly, people have spoken of the difficulties of their experience, be that to do with race or gender or any number of reasons, only to be told by someone who has never shared that experience how wrong they are about it.

There was a story I was once told when I was in Zimbabwe, about a charity that came to a village to build a school for the local children. Over and over again, the local population tried to speak to the charity and explain that there were several other projects that would be more helpful to them than a school – like fixing the local well. The charity explained to them how education would free their children from the poverty-cycle and enable them to forge a brighter future. They were insistent on this and the project was completed. The villagers still had no clean water source, but they did have a big, new school building. The charity left the village, but it turned out they had neither trained nor recruited any teachers, nor provided any books or pencils. There was no capacity actually to use the building as it was intended, and so it fell into disrepair. I don't doubt this was all done with the best of intentions. Still, it shows how a great deal of work can be put into something (the school) that should logically achieve a desirable outcome (increased number of children in primary education), but without an understanding of other key factors (lack of teachers and educational resources).

Guilt

In this example, it is very clear how damaging such a mindset can be, but the reality is that in the aid sector it is a serious and insidious problem, often caught up with feelings of sympathy, which can have complex outcomes, including feelings of pity which can lead to 'othering' and to patronising behaviours as well as a sense of 'we know best'. Frequently, I saw the attitude that if people were trying to do the right thing, they were therefore above criticism – even from the people they were apparently trying to help. But you cannot, and should not, justify poor outcomes by good intentions, as it usually exposes a flawed logic in project planning. I did worry about this, and about the right way to be useful. I certainly didn't want to help simply for the sake of being helpful, or for the satisfaction it might bring me, but I also worried that it was wrong to be at home enjoying life when I knew there were others out there who couldn't.

To be honest, I wasn't very happy with the way I was living my life. I loved being with my friends again, but I definitely drank too much, and after the first couple of dates with people I met through dating apps, the novelty wore off slightly. I was, perhaps, behaving exactly as everyone would expect a 'normal' person in her late twenties to be behaving, and yet it felt entirely alien. There were momentary fragments of joy, floating on a sea of malaise. I felt that I was making mistakes left, right and centre. I felt that I was breaking everything that I had built within me.

I really do wonder whether those years with HALO created such a sustained feeling of being out of my depth that it felt unnatural to be in a position of comfort. Working for HALO was interesting in that way, in that however accomplished you might be, you were always stretched somehow, whether in constantly striving to keep on top of the technical side, or in trying to acclimatise to a new country and to the unique challenges presented by that particular programme. If I'm honest, nearly always your job with HALO could credibly have required two people rather than one.

The best thing about that time in London was undoubtedly my friends. Living with my girlfriends again was such a wonderful experience. I wish now that I had been more open with them about how I was feeling, but I think I was afraid to push them away at a time when I needed them close. I needed that human contact and familiarity. I needed to watch ridiculous TV with them. I needed to drink warm white wine on a Friday night. I needed to sit with my legs tucked under someone else's, and my head resting on the shoulder of the person next to me. I needed to tie my greasy hair up on a Sunday morning, and come out of my room to a kitchen filled with cups of tea and love. I desperately needed to be close to people. To me, at that time, the impulse was to be physically close. To snuggle together under a duvet on the sofa. Now, however, I don't think it was really about that at all. I think I confused physical closeness with emotional closeness – and we were certainly emotionally close, although I never really let any of them in to see how I was thinking or feeling at that time. I did mention to them, on occasions, that I was struggling to sleep, but I never managed to go beyond that. In particular, I never really discussed the guilt I was feeling. I had a sense of both frustration and uselessness that I didn't know how to explain without their having seen and experienced some of the things I had over the preceding years.

My friends have always supported me, but I am not an easy person to support. When I went to work abroad, I announced that I was leaving, then disappeared and rarely messaged while I was away. I know this was self-preservation, that I avoided certain forms of social media because it was making me upset; maybe we've all had a little taste of that from the COVID-19 lockdown period, when we were taunted by the 'Memories' features of Facebook and Instagram, and reminded that last year we were on holiday, or sitting in a beer garden. Sometimes it's easier just not to see it at all. Friendship is not a one-sided arrangement, though. A part of the reason why I felt so removed is because I didn't keep up to date with everything, because I didn't send messages or cards at life milestones. Those months in London were a chance to reconnect, and in some ways I did. I caught up on who was who, and all the new ways our group fitted together, but I didn't really tell anyone how I was feeling.

Sometimes it was enough; it was enough for Cassie to hold me in a tight hug when she could see I needed it. It was enough when Bessie and I would meet for a Peroni in the local pub, and she would laugh as I tried to put a positive spin on a story, and we would talk about the things we felt we still didn't know about life. It was enough to nip outside for a cigarette with Stef, and laugh into the darkness about the ridiculous date I had just been on. And it was enough to bake potatoes with Steph in the kitchen, and have her reassure me when I burnt the beans in the bottom of the pan. It was enough to share M&S chocolate puddings with Jess, while laughing our way through an episode of *Gavin & Stacey*. It was enough to come home and laugh with Emily about my latest Hollywood bikini wax, or have her coach me on how to be confident for a date, only for me to drink three-quarters of a bottle of amaretto on the tube there, and arrive at a BYOC (bring your own cocktails) date with barely enough left to make a cocktail.

Of course, this was enough – it was more than enough. It's just that I didn't let it filter down to a deeper level. Beneath that top layer of comfort spent in the company of my friends, in my own head I continued to berate and punish myself, and that part of me was quite alone. I was good at acting as though I was fine, and a large part of that was because I held people at arm's length so that they couldn't see what was going on, so they couldn't see the destructive sides of me, the person that made mistakes. Out at arm's length I could hold and support someone as a friend, without their needing to see any of the darkness inside of me. Concealing too much darkness within yourself only ever serves to make you feel that you are the worst person ever, because you are missing the human connection you need to see: that those around you are just like you.

On the morning I went to Afghanistan, I left for the airport before anyone had woken up. On the table in the kitchen, I laid out small friendship bracelets for everyone. This was so typical of me. I could have (and should have) spoken to them, I could have thanked them in person, given each of them a bracelet, but firstly I didn't want to make a fuss out of leaving and, secondly, I knew I couldn't have done it, I couldn't have said in person the things I would have wanted to say. So I slipped away before anyone was up, leaving a pile of possessions from my London life in my sister's attic.

I never reclaimed those things. I never lived that life again, because in the space of the next year I would go from Afghanistan to *Love Island*.

Chapter 6

Storytellers

───

In Afghanistan, I joined the Danish Demining Group – the Human Security Unit under the Danish Refugee Council – as deputy programme manager. This later changed slightly, however, as alongside carrying out that role, I took on that of armed violence reduction manager to assist in the delivery of armed violence reduction (AVR) components of a new FCO-funded pilot project to help build up the resilience of vulnerable communities and the rehabilitation of returnees and IDPs (internally displaced persons).

Working in Afghanistan was fascinating, and the country itself is particularly beautiful. Of course, I knew there were some risks associated with Afghanistan, but, if I'm honest, I was excited more than anything else. I had only ever heard from people who worked there how great it was, not only because the work is really interesting, but because of the stunning scenery; and everyone raved about the food, lots of which is cooked in ghee (a clarified butter), imparting a delicious, buttery, almost sweet flavour. I was lucky in a way in that my perception of Afghanistan as a place had not been shaped by news reports, but rather by personal experiences, and I suppose that also, by that point, I was very used to packing up my bag and heading off to a new place without knowing what to expect – in fact, I enjoyed that sense of venturing into the unknown.

There were of course various security considerations that had to be taken into account – first of all, it was important to dress appropriately. For women, this meant that even if you were wearing trousers, you should still be covered to your knees. I would wear long tunic shirts over work trousers, and usually a grey headscarf. Inside the office in Kabul, you could take your headscarf off, but anywhere outside the office buildings we kept our heads covered at all times.

Shortly after I arrived, an Australian woman working for another NGO was kidnapped in Kabul. A couple of my friends, former colleagues at HALO, were shot at while visiting ammunition stores on the city outskirts, including the man who had conducted some of my EOD training. A rogue policeman shot and killed a man working for a security company as he passed through Kabul airport, which we used to travel into and out of the country. So all in all, the security situation wasn't great, and tensions were running high. Non-locals working for the DRC (Danish Refugee Council) were mainly confined to our compound, which contained both the living quarters and the main office, all within a barbed-wire-topped wall. Any time we left, we carried GPS trackers wherever we went, hidden in any discreet pocket we had (I kept mine in the inner pocket of my cargo-style work trousers). The hope was that if you were taken, your abductors wouldn't find it until the team had managed to locate you. Or at the very least, they would have some indication of where you were picked up, and maybe even where you were taken to. On arrival at the compound, you received a security briefing from DRC's in-country head of security, during which we were told the best way to protect ourselves was to maintain a low profile; not standing out minimised the risk faced. Not making yourself a target is probably the first rule of security in general: it's best not to attract attention to yourself.

There was a phone system to which all the staff mobile phones we were issued with on arrival were signed up, and you would receive text messages whenever an explosion went off in the city, giving you the location and initial details of the attack. It was a time when the use of IEDs was widespread, so drivers and gate security guards were equipped with a device that looked like a giant version of a dentist's mirror. It consisted of a circular mirror attached to the cranked end of a telescopic handle, allowing the guards to look beneath a vehicle to check whether any device had been attached to the underside while it was parked. Text messages warning of explosions were pretty regular, but of course these alerts covered the whole city, and were not limited to IED attacks, so they also reported gas leaks, fires, and so on. Kabul is divided into numbered districts, and the warning text messages would give you an idea of the location of the explosion. If one was recorded near our compound, there would be a quick check to see where we all were, and to make sure we were safe.

One evening, while working at the desk in my room, I heard one of these explosions go off a few hundred metres from the compound. There was an immediate check to ensure everyone was safe. Everyone in the office was fine, but it turned out that some relations of a staff member had been killed in the attack. Each of us kept a helmet and a flak jacket in our bedrooms in the compound. The bottom floor of the building was a safe floor, with reinforced walls and radio communications. If anything happened, we were to put on the flak jacket and helmet, and head downstairs to the safe floor, and we attended regular sessions simulating this kind of evacuation for when it might be needed.

We were very restricted in how much we could travel, but I did go on a few outings while I was there, and I loved driving through Kabul. It's a spectacular city, unlike anything I had seen before. For anyone who has never seen it, Kabul is immensely striking, located as it is in a valley in the Hindu Kush mountains. The skyline is formed of dramatic peaks, that seem to plunge into the hustle and bustle of the city. Houses cling to even the steepest slopes, and at night the light from these homes gives the illusion of a starry skyline, rather than a starry sky.

One of the trips I was allowed to make was to our explosives stores, kept in a series of bunkers as required by the Afghan government. On the drive there, we went past the monument that had been built in memory of Farkhunda. Many people will have heard about her horrific murder when it made international news in March 2015. Farkhunda Malikzada was a twenty-seven-year-old volunteer teacher. On her way home from class on 19 March, she stopped by a shrine in central Kabul. While she was there, she saw a fortune-teller selling good-luck charms,[7] which she disapproved of as she believed they contravened the guidance of the Islamic faith, and took advantage of women – the charms tended to be small pieces of paper on which were written wishes for such things as marriage or pregnancy. Typically, these were bought by women, to keep in their pocket as talismans for good fortune.

Farkhunda made her disapproval known to the shrine's custodian, who, enraged by her complaints about the fortune-teller, falsely accused her of burning the Qur'an. Standing at the gates to the shrine, he shouted the accusation at her again and again until a crowd began to gather. They dragged Farkhunda from the shrine and began to beat her. The police arrived and initially fired gunshots into the air, and the crowd momentarily stood back from the terrified woman. Her headscarf had fallen off leaving her long dark hair framing her blood-covered face. But the police then stood back, and the mob descended again. Farkhunda screamed in pain as she was repeatedly kicked and beaten with sticks, her body beginning to convulse as the horrific attack went on and on. A man ran her over with his car, dragging her body for hundreds of metres. Eventually she was thrown into the dry riverbed, where the mob threw stones at her. Finally, they set her on fire.

---

[7] https://www.nytimes.com/2015/12/27/world/asia/flawed-justice-after-a-mob-killed-an-afghan-woman.html?_r=0

Her clothes were so drenched in blood that they would not burn and so they used their own clothing to ignite the flames.[8]

At first, many prominent Afghan figures condoned the attack, despite harrowing footage of Farkhunda's torture and murder, which had been filmed on mobile phones by many of those present (including men who had participated in the attack), and disseminated online. Her mother had to go to the mortuary to identify her daughter's body, and had to watch online the terrible ordeal her daughter had endured. She had to watch her daughter beg for help, covered in blood as police officers stood by and did nothing. Farkhunda's family were told that it had been proven that she had burnt the Qur'an and that police had been unable to protect her; they were advised to leave Kabul for their own safety.[9] A mob had brutally beaten a defenceless young woman to death, and yet initially she was the pariah rather than the victim.

The President of Afghanistan, Ashraf Ghani, ordered an investigation, and it quickly became evident that the claims that Farkhunda had burnt the Qur'an were entirely false. Several prominent officials retracted their statements, and a national outcry against the attack ensued; thirteen police officers were suspended, and twenty-eight men arrested and sent for trial. At Farkhunda's funeral, the coffin was carried by women, the first time in Afghan history that women had served as pallbearers. They refused to let any man touch it.

---

[8] https://www.nytimes.com/2015/12/27/world/asia/flawed-justice-after-a-mob-killed-an-afghan-woman.html

[9] https://www.nytimes.com/2015/12/27/world/asia/flawed-justice-after-a-mob-killed-an-afghan-woman.html

The national revulsion against the crime was seen as a seminal moment in the protection of women's rights in Afghanistan, and initially it seemed some kind of justice would be served. Women's rights groups campaigned for justice for Farkhunda, and for the rights of all women subjected to violence. The trial was reported upon internationally and it was hoped this would mark a new era in safeguarding human rights, although it was evident that in order for any meaningful progress to be made, the judicial process would need to be seen to be measured and appropriate.

In the end, forty-nine men, including nineteen police officers, stood trial in May 2015 over Farkhunda's death. Some members of the mob who appeared in the footage were never charged. While the complexity of such a murder case is evident, the investigation, that omitted to follow up on video evidence showing those involved, is not the only perplexing detail of the judicial process. Four men received the death penalty, including the man who had originally created the false story about the burning of the Qur'an. Later, all four death sentences were commuted in closed trials, three of the sentences were reduced to twenty years' imprisonment, and the fourth to ten years, the final man arguing that he was just seventeen years old at the time of the attack, although others say he was twenty.[10]

To try to ensure that this is not a one-sided account, I must concede that the legal system floundered under the increasing public pressure surrounding the case, and there was a huge

---

[10] www.nytimes.com/2015/12/27/world/asia/flawed-justice-after-a-mob-killed-an-afghan-woman.html

variation in how different people believed those involved should be dealt with. Many of those accused did not have lawyers, and they were only given a few moments each to speak in defence of themselves. Some who were accused later turned out not to have been present at all. Although a huge amount of funding has been poured into the judicial system and legal training in Afghanistan by the United States as well as various European countries, all too often this has lacked an appreciation of deep-rooted Afghan beliefs. It is axiomatic that all justice systems are imperfect, and the Western ideal is certainly not the faultless solution that it may appear to be. The flaws in implementing such training in Afghanistan were two-fold: firstly, it was an attempt to integrate a flawed system with a flawed system; secondly, it sought to conduct such integration using training methods that took into account the skills and values of the Western rule-of-law, rather than of those to be taught – for example, age is considered extremely important in Afghanistan when it comes to those who are considered authority figures. To bring in a young, bright Western lawyer with excellent teaching skills may seem like an effective plan, but it disregards important and consequential social norms that will impact how seriously the training is taken.

Although the very fact a trial was held was seen as a mark of success for some, many felt the investigation and subsequent trials did not truly hold the guilty to account, and left a precedent for violence against women to continue.

The memorial to Farkhunda stands where her body was finally burnt, and I would pass it many more times before I left

Afghanistan. Her tragic death set in motion a series of events that brought hope to women nationally and internationally. Afghanistan remains one of the most dangerous places in the world in which to be a woman, but none the less she fought to live with dignity and respect, which would have taken immense courage throughout her all too short life. Having that courage brings many difficult moments as well, for you are seeking a better future that you know could exist but have no idea when, or even if, it ever will. Farkhunda was brave in the face of odds that were stacked against her from birth, and in being so she brought a whole new belief to the hearts of so many.

Some days after another trip past the Farkhunda memorial, I was sitting at the table in the main room of the living quarters in the compound, watching BBC World News, as the results of the 2016 US presidential election were repeated over and over again. I looked on open-mouthed as the programme showed clips of Donald Trump's victory speech. I could barely believe it. I had talked about the upcoming election with friends back home, and occasionally with my colleagues in Kabul, and to be honest I don't think any of us had seriously entertained the possibility of him winning. I had operated within an echo chamber that mirrored my views of him: we had fed our belief that Hillary Clinton would win through looking at the evidence that supported that assertion, and at the polls that fed the narrative that she would win. That was what I was expecting. I had not even the slightest inkling that Trump might gain power.

The world felt irreparably off balance. As individuals, people often feel overwhelmed by the world's problems, not knowing what they can do to help. Everything seems contradictory, and too complex ever to yield a straight answer as to the right way to live. Historically, we have solved this problem by working in or with large groups and structures, which allows us to assimilate the information and, on occasions, democratically identify the right path. Even when groups have leaders, we often take comfort in pack mentality, which takes away some of the burden of decision-making. The idea that, as individuals, each of us can make sense of the world, particularly one that is becoming ever more complex, is terrifying. And that is why, to me, Trump was most terrifying. Here was a man who thought he had all the answers, and who would brook no questioning or challenges. Who had simplified the world down to his level of comprehension, so that he believed himself capable of understanding complex processes, people and systems. Ultimately, what had taught him to believe this was a world that was shaped to his advantage, in which he could reduce or conflate ideas to suit his conclusion.

Farkhunda's story is important to so many people. The reason I have related it here was because passing her memorial was something that made me think every single time. I was twenty-seven years old at the time, the same age as Farkhunda was when she was killed. When we hear accounts of suffering, we are all too often advised to keep a measured distance between ourselves and that pain. We are told to maintain our calm, and not take it personally. But it is personal. Attacks on different genders, race or class are attacks against humanity.

The playing field is not even. There are many of us who have begun to benefit from a seemingly more equitable society, but the advances we have felt do not necessarily trickle down in the way it is suggested that they do. In fact, it takes a concerted effort from those of us who feel we have begun to benefit from this more equitable society, to translate that into meaningful change for others. Often, those who have already experienced such benefits already have a more stable platform from which to campaign for rights for various groups, whether they belong to these groups or not. When we do belong to them, we can feel more justified in expressing our feelings about those rights, but even then we may be complicit in a flawed system that frequently means those of us with greater rights or power 'give a voice' to those with fewer rights. This is a paradox, because surely the person best placed to inform others is the one who shares that experience, and yet our lopsided society means the loudest voices are often those with the least to say. Time and again, we hear how we must give a voice to the 'voiceless', but I don't believe that is the right term to use at all. People have a voice, what they may not have is a viable route to the audience they deserve, because as much as we all have a part to play, there is no doubt that there are central figures orchestrating who and what deserves our time and attention. And these 'conductors' undoubtedly influence the voices we hear. The violinist may think she is performing out of choice, but she is still being kept to time by an overarching power.

In fact, the easiest way to 'give' people a voice is to ask them a question, and provide a forum in which they can answer, on their own terms. This is immensely important in the world of humanitarian aid, where all too frequently I saw misguided projects that had not taken into account the needs and knowledge of the people it was hoped they would help. I remember being told about one project in Afghanistan in which women were educated in avoiding violence. In order to teach them about their rights, they first learned about them, and then put on a play about why they should not be subjected to violence. Except that, because this was Afghanistan, men were not allowed to watch the play – only women. Of course cultural appropriateness must be taken into account, but what troubled me about this project was the idea that women were going home with this new information, and potentially being put at risk by trying to enforce such knowledge within an environment where the perpetrator of such violence not only had not received the same training, but would in any case have had to change his entire mindset. You cannot ask victims to become educators, because the power imbalance does not allow them to share the knowledge safely. (I should add that there are charities that do this work differently and do incorporate male stakeholders; this was just one example that I heard about.)

It is not that I disagree with the medium – plays are often used as a means to exemplify laws or moral codes, and there is a lot to be said for speaking to victims, explaining their rights to them, and empowering them with knowledge, but to place someone in further danger is irresponsible. To me, this was the absolute distillation of the concept of 'giving someone a voice'; to put them in a play to act out the rules society had said were acceptable but with little thought given to safeguarding those who were worst affected by violence.

I take it personally. I get wound up when things are unfair, or ill thought-out. What I do take from that experience is that we must learn how to be actively involved in amplifying and empowering the voices so that the way we move through the world is informed by all those around us – not just those with the greatest power to speak. That we look at our beliefs, and contemplate how they fit within a framework of intersectionality. That we consider what it means to have privilege and power, and how we use that in communicating with others. That we look behind social frameworks that inform us through the prism of someone else's gaze. That we ask questions of the person who can give us the answers rather than the powerful person who is telling their story for them.

Because now we know how dangerous it can be when a man stands at the gates of a shrine, and tells the story of a young woman.

Chapter 7

Imposter Island

I landed back in the UK, and went home to Scotland, completely unsure of what to do next. I had moved to London the year previously, and that hadn't worked out as planned. I hadn't reconnected with my friends the way I expected to, and I had still felt like I was out of place. When I left for Afghanistan, I had not realised how fragile my mental state was, and I was still unable to get over the unnerving numbness I felt. I couldn't realistically stay at home in Scotland for ever, but I hoped that there might be some future in taking shorter contracts and balancing life between the two, but this was not certain at the time. I considered completing a law conversion course and trying to transition into more of an advocacy type position. And then I received a message from a person whose name I did not recognise:

Not the Type

> Hi Camilla! Hope you're well! This is a little random but I'm currently casting on a primetime ITV show and would love to chat to you regarding a potential TV opportunity. Let me know if you would be interested in finding out more. Best wishes, Nikita

I had no idea which show this would be for at that stage, and I was never told, and to this day still don't know the reason why I was contacted in the first place. I responded with an email address and received a reply with a few more details and a number to call (incidentally, the message was flagged by my email service provider as 'dangerous'). It did initially feel like a bit of a hoax, but we arranged to speak on the telephone and it ended up being an interesting conversation. I was invited to drop by the ITV studios in London for an informal meeting. Since I was already coming down to see friends it was pretty easy to fit in, and I didn't see the harm. From what I remember, I'm not even sure if at that stage I knew what show it was, or whether they told me that in the meeting. I met with Lewis and Nikita, and had a very pleasant and comfortingly normal chat. I don't even remember having to answer many questions about my love life! Our talk was more about my family, my work and my thoughts about the show, which they told me was *Love Island*.

That meeting was the first time I had properly laughed at things in months. It was the first time I had sat and talked and felt noticed and understood. It was also nice just to have distraction from my own thoughts for a while. I think it lasted about an hour and then I left and I remember feeling relieved. I was invited to come meet them again when they were up in Scotland holding an invited audition day, for a similar conversation but this time on camera. I honestly think that if they had led with this, I probably wouldn't have gone to that second meeting, but because I had already met them I felt much less wary. I didn't have a great many nice clothes at this time, so I wore exactly the same outfit that I had worn to the first chat in London, and worried that they might think I had no clothes.

A few weeks after the filmed chat they contacted me again, this time about meeting the executive producers and going through the fitness to participate assessment for the show. This was the final stage in the process. If the 'execs' liked you then they put you forward to the channel as part of the proposed line-up, and ultimately they have the final say. Having realised I didn't have anything to wear to this meeting with the execs either, and now with a chance of being selected for the show, I sold a load of stuff on eBay and bought a few new outfits from Zara, just in case.

It must have been a few weeks later that Lewis called me. I was out walking my parents' dog, and it was incredibly windy (typical Scottish weather), but through the wind I heard him say that they wanted me to be in the opening cast. It didn't sink in straight away. Even though I had been invited to the last stage in the process – the meeting with the execs that I mention above – in all honesty I didn't really think that they would pick me. I thought my answers to a few of the questions were pretty poor, and having seen the answers in the opening interviews of previous series, I didn't think I was similar to the strong characters they usually picked.

I went home, and had a crumpet with some peanut butter. My parents' dog is called Crumpet, and we were in the habit of getting back from his afternoon walk and sitting on the sofa together, sharing a crumpet and reading a book.[11] I had felt very down during this period. I came back from Afghanistan overwhelmed by guilt, and rightly so. The more insight I gained into the real world, the more I saw power dynamics that worked in my favour, and the more I questioned my role, and where I would be most useful. I was utterly confused about how to move forward with my life. I didn't feel as if I had processed the past, nor did I have any comprehension of a future 'happier' version of myself. The *Love Island* application was just going on in the background. It seems very different now when I write it, but the reality was just the odd phone call now and then. I suppose that if I had been really desperate to get on the show, then maybe it would have been different, but truthfully I just felt very lucky with each round that passed, but it didn't dominate my life. What had dominated my life was the big question of what to do next, and now, suddenly, there was a defined answer. It wasn't an answer I would have expected, and I hadn't found it for myself, but it felt like something that I could keep my eyes fixed on, and it kept me looking forwards rather than back.

I had genuinely considered saying no. I think Lewis might

[11] Sorry, Dad, I know he isn't allowed crumpets, or to sit on the sofa, and yes that is why he was so badly behaved by the time I left!

have known this, because he was very careful in managing our discussions after the conversation in which he confirmed they would like me to be part of the opening cast. In fact, the whole team were. He asked me to travel down to London in about a week, for two days to take the press shots, film my interview (the one you see in the first episode), and then, on the following day, to film the opening of the first episode of *Love Island*, when the viewers see the contestants leaving their jobs to come to the island. I was so nervous to be around the production team, because they all seemed so confident, all of them were very funny and smart. They are also all great friends with each other, and I always get nervous in situations where a friendship group is already established. In fact, they were extremely welcoming. I was looked after by Coco, one of the brightest, warmest people I've ever met. She is legendary behind the scenes of *Love Island* not only for being very good at her job, but also for her humour and her ability to put people at ease.

When I first arrived at the shoot day, I met her and Mike, series producer on the show. I recently met up with Mike for lunch, (he was actually the person who created the stunning *La La Land*-themed final date that I went on with Jamie). We were talking about that very first shoot day, when we took the press shots for the show, and how uncomfortable I had been. He made me laugh so much when he told me how he had basically had to put in a furtive radio call to check that I knew which show I was going on, after I wouldn't come out from behind the screens when trying on the bikini they had found for me! I didn't really have many bikini options with me, and they had a silver one in wardrobe which they thought might be a nice fit, so they asked me to try it on. Off I went behind the screens and in due course called out that I had it on. There were a couple of minutes of awkward silence and then Mike said, 'Er, are you actually going to come out and show us?'

I think that day was so alien to me that, instead of being a shock to the system, it just felt altogether surreal. I couldn't quite work out how much of my discomfort was to do with my own insecurities about changing in front of people and posing in a bikini, and how much was to do with how different life had been for the last few years. It felt bizarre to go from covering up in Afghanistan, to posing in a silver bikini for *Love Island*. My qualms on the shoot day were echoed in the first few days of the programme, when my need for privacy while changing, and my reluctance to take off an overshirt that I wore on top of my bikini in the first couple of days, prompted a greater feeling of discomfort, and perhaps reflection about whether I really should be there.

After the first shoot day, I went in the evening to meet the two of my friends who had agreed to manage my Instagram account. You obviously don't have access to your phone or social media while you are in the villa, and so it seemed prudent to ask someone to keep an eye on it for me. We did not at that stage realise how big *Love Island* was going to get that year, and I hadn't left them with any instructions bar keep an eye on it, and if you have time feel free to post now and again but don't feel any pressure to. We ate noodles at a shared table in a dark restaurant, and laughed about the

Returning to Cambodia to film *What Camilla Did Next*, November 2018.

(Photo © SandStone Global Productions Ltd)

Above left: Camilla (right) with her older and younger sisters.

Centre right: And (right) with her sisters and younger brother.

Below: Camilla (right) with her mother, brother, younger sister, older sister and father.

Above left: Camilla in Cambodia in November 2013. *(Photo © Sophal Try)*

Centre right: And at a training ground in January 2014. Cambodia was her first posting with HALO.

Below left: Sheltering in a military bunker during the HALO training course in Nagorno-Karabakh in April 2015.

Below right: It's not just landmines – Camilla servicing a Toyota Land Cruiser during the same course in Nagorno-Karabakh.

Scenes from HALO Phase 1 Training in Nagorno-Karabakh, January–April 2015.

Above left: The HALO team at the campsite during the Malhazine UEMS (unplanned explosions at munition sites) task in Maputo, Mozambique.

Centre right: 'Quiet, firing.' Using the radio to check the cordon before detonating a demolition charge with a Beethoven firer. Maputo, Mozambique.

Below left: Cautiously excavating an R2M2 pressure-operated anti-personnel mine during my first attempt at the 'lifting' drill in Zimbabwe, June 2015.

Below right: Zimbabwe: carefully removing the detonator from the side of an MAPS pressure-operated anti-personnel landmine (see pages 75–6).

Above left: *Love Island* contestants arriving back from the island, July 2017 – Camilla and Jamie at right.
(Photo © Beretta/Sims/ Shutterstock)

Centre right: My friends greeting me at the airport with a banner, July 2017.

Below left and right: At the annual Everyday Heroes Awards in London, September 2017 – not always comfortable with the limelight.
(Photos © Nils Jorgensen/Shutterstock)

Above left: Joining Lord (Alf) Dubs (second from left) and others outside the House of Lords.

Above right: Speaking on a panel with the Choose Love/Help Refugees team in December 2017.

Above: Volunteering in Greece with Jamie, August 2017.

Jamie with Gus, Camilla with Audrey, March 2019.

unlikeliness of the whole thing, but they never warned me off or discouraged me from making the decision to go on *Love Island*. I am lucky in that I have an open-minded group of friends anyway, and they were used to my making seemingly bizarre choices, like flitting off to Cambodia at a moment's notice. They were helpful and supportive, and reassured me that they would be watching the show, and also that they would be there for me no matter what happened (which they all were, even to the point of waiting to meet me at the airport when we landed back in the UK after the show).

The next morning I joined part of the production team again to film the 'leaving for the island' scene. I was particularly worried about the vision they had for this. We went to a paintball park in Essex, and a guy came with a big Land Rover for me to drive. What bothered me was that the whole place felt a bit military-themed; even the outfit I was wearing included a helmet, something I rarely wore while demining – only a few types of protective visor have a helmet attached, it is more normal to wear a visor with a headband. I really didn't want to come across as though I had been in the military, because in the humanitarian sector the importance of being neutral, and of working with a humanitarian imperative, is drummed into you. The military have a completely different task, and thus undergo very different training and have different goals. I didn't want anyone in the humanitarian sector to think that I was behaving inappropriately, and I *really* didn't want anyone in the military to think that I was pretending I had any connection to that world, or any experience of what it is like.

Not the Type

I had to drive the Land Rover backwards and forwards many times, each time stopping the vehicle, opening the door, climbing out, taking off my helmet and shaking out my hair. This was truly my worst nightmare. There were about ten people watching, and I just can't take myself seriously in a situation like that. I felt very awkward and self-conscious and I also felt so sorry for the team filming it, as I could see they were getting frustrated. I mean, how hard is it to get out of a vehicle and shake your hair around? Apparently, for me, nearly impossible. In addition to that, I was becoming anxious about how military the shoot felt. Once the film crew finally had something usable, I went and spoke to Coco about it. She promised to pass on my feedback to the executive producers, and then I caught the train back up to Scotland. During the journey, Andy, one of the executive producers, called me to talk about my concerns about the shoot. He seemed to understand where I was coming from, and also assured me that what had been filmed really was just a flash of footage to introduce me, something that you don't realise when you have been filming for most of the morning. The interview we had recorded the day before was, he said, the main way viewers would get to know us. I felt reassured, and, to be honest, even people I knew well found my job as a deminer hard to understand, so I could see the difficulty in conveying it to a TV audience.

I think this was probably the day when it all started to feel more real. I arrived home, and began to get very nervous about what I had got myself into. All the slow-mo filming had reminded me how uncomfortable I can feel and I worried that I wouldn't be like the other people on the show. I felt that the team from the show had to be particularly attentive to me throughout in order to make me comfortable, but that maybe for everyone else it was easier. This feeling was based solely on what I had picked up during the two days, but in truth, there was no way I could have known how everyone else dealt with that experience, whether they found it as overwhelming or nerve-racking as I did.

There is considerable speculation about the cast-holding period before *Love Island*. What actually happens is that your chaperone picks you up from your home in the UK, and takes you to the nearest airport, from where you both fly out to Mallorca. Each person is accommodated somewhere in Mallorca, although obviously none of you are in the same hotel. Each time you go out for dinner or to the shops, your chaperone messages the others to make sure you won't bump into anyone else from the programme. It is true that your phone is taken away, and the main reason for that is so you won't see who the other Islanders are, when they are announced in the press, as this happens in the days prior to the start of the show. During the cast-holding period, we had one shoot that was for the opening credits, for which we did our own makeup and wore our own swimwear. It was carefully orchestrated, so that each future Islander arrived and left the shoot location, without bumping into any of the other future Islanders. A huge amount of effort is put into ensuring no one meets before that first day in the villa.

There were various regulations and guidelines that had to be followed as part of participating in the show. We were

171

allowed one washbag with toiletries, and one makeup bag, and all items had to fit into one case. We couldn't take in anything sharp, so if you needed scissors or anything, you had to request them in the Beach Hut – a small room in the villa with a chair and a camera. The Beach Hut is where you see contestants talking straight to camera in a diary-style manner. The show did not have a clothes sponsor that year (I believe they do normally have one now), which meant that we all just ended up sharing the clothes we had each brought in, so that we had different things to wear each evening. We were asked to dress up in the evenings, mainly so that viewers would understand the passage of time, and when certain conversations and events took place. This was all explained to us individually by our respective chaperones in advance of our going into the villa. It was also explained that at the very maximum we would be allowed two measures of alcohol a night. One unit was either two small cans of beer, one glass of white or rosé wine, or one glass of prosecco. Some nights we wouldn't receive any, and if any night seemed to be getting out of hand, and we had already received one measure of alcohol, they would not put the second in the larder, which was in the kitchen and had two separate entry doors. One could be accessed by the Islanders, and one opened to outside the villa and could be accessed by crew. Food, and any other items we needed would be placed in the larder by the crew, but if a crew member was in there, the door that could be accessed by the Islanders was locked so that we couldn't go in there at the same time.

On the day we were to enter, each Islander was taken

separately by their chaperone to a hotel near the villa, where we were to get ready. We were all put in separate rooms to get ready, and you weren't allowed to leave in case you bumped into anyone in the corridor. There was some confusion over timings, and I actually didn't find out the time I was meant to leave (around midday) until about an hour before, so it ended up being a bit of a rush, especially because we were then subjected to a final security check of our bags to make sure we were not taking in anything that we weren't meant to have.

You are then taken by your chaperone to the location of the villa. Although the hotel was close to it, I recall that the drive still took about forty minutes, during which time I became more and more nervous. When we arrived, our chaperone took us into a small tent at the foot of a steep drive with the villa visible in the background. Each of us was in a separate tent so that we didn't meet before going in. It was bizarre knowing that the next person was in the tent just metres from my own. We were moved through the tents as each new person went into the villa, and then it was my turn to enter. I was put in one car and taken up close to the entrance, and then transferred into one of the open-top vehicles that you see in Episode 1 of *Love Island*. I was told to look excited and happy, and I really tried to, but I was so nervous. I remember very little after that, apart from someone opening the prosecco, and my promptly spilling a glass all down my front, then panicking that this would be the first thing caught on camera!

So that is how I found myself, a few months after returning

from Kabul, standing among the opening cast of *Love Island* 2017, being told about the rules of 'coupling up'. The contrast was palpable. I had gone from an environment where every day I was covered from head to toe, to being somewhere where it was more common to wear a bikini all day than anything else. The key wasn't to blend in, it was to stand out – something I did not feel I could do.

On our second day in the villa, it rained badly and they had to cover all the cameras with protective shrouds and were unable to film. We were all collected inside, and chaperoned to ensure nothing happened (so that the viewer wouldn't miss anything) while we waited for the rain to stop. A few of us went for a nap in the bedroom, and everyone else stayed in the living room. Just as I was dropping off, I thought I heard a snippet of conversation from the other room that sounded like 'Why is she here, it seems like she didn't know about the show…' They could have been talking about anyone or anything, or I might have misheard, or it may never have been said at all. I have to say, though, that if it was said in relation to me, I was rather on their side. My overwhelming memory of the first few days of *Love Island* was feeling like an imposter. This was not unfamiliar territory for me – I've always felt like an outsider, and this was just another iteration of that. In the first few days, everyone around me seemed more attractive, more interesting, more confident and funnier than me. I felt like an outsider on *Love Island*, even though I was quite literally in it!

Certainly, when I first left the villa, I saw that many of the online comments about me from the early days questioned why I was there (some in a more positive way than others). I can understand that perception, because it is exactly the way I felt about it. I questioned why I was there. I wondered if it was just the vacuum of the last few months that had landed me in such an unlikely situation. Ostensibly, I'd gone on *Love Island* hoping that it would help with building my confidence in social situations. More selfishly, I needed a distraction from the way I'd been thinking and feeling, and here was an answer.

It was definitely an escape, in a manner of speaking, but it didn't feel that I was running away because the prospect of seven weeks socialising on camera was such a terrifying one. I think perhaps that knowing how much I felt I had got out of experiences where I had felt out of my depth before, I believed that this would be similarly rewarding since it was just as terrifying to me, if not more so. But in those first few days, I was part fascinated, part terrified. I was so overwhelmed I asked to leave. For the most part, we were called to the Beach Hut to talk, but if you needed anything, you could go there and speak to someone. You were technically talking to a camera, but the voices behind it were friendly and reassuring. Shortly afterwards, we received 'a text' stating that there would be recoupling in the next few days.

For those who don't know, recoupling is when you have the opportunity to pair up with your love interest. Usually there will be either one or two more men, or one or two more women, and whichever group has fewer people does the picking, leaving someone unpicked who is then 'dumped' from the Island. This happens at regular intervals throughout the seven weeks. In the meantime, 'bombshells' are also introduced into the villa at regular intervals. 'Bombshells' are new singletons, who are introduced with the express intention of shaking things up, so that the couples continue to change throughout the season.

Before that first recoupling there were six women and five men, and I was very confident I wouldn't be picked, and so could leave quietly, go home, and remember *Love Island* as a crazy mistake. Except that what actually happened was that two new bombshells, Jonny and Chris, were brought in before it took place, meaning there was an extra man rather than an extra woman. So I ended up staying. Not only that, but on the first night Jonny and Chris were brought in, I received a 'text' saying the public had voted for me to go on a date with Jonny. This show of support surprised me, and perhaps I interpreted this as the viewers not seeing me as being as much of an outsider as I saw myself. Either way, I had to some extent settled in during the first few days, and had got over the hideous memories of when I had first gone to boarding school and felt overwhelmingly like the odd one out. Montana and Gabby made a particular effort to include me, and propped me up during my crisis of confidence.

I think about that time a lot. It was a situation so similar to when you first go to school, or university, or even start a new job. Wherever there is a group of people, they will naturally form sub-groups and ally themselves with those with whom they most obviously share common ground. The problem is if you are shy or initially quiet, you miss that bonding phase. Often there will be things you would have in common, but you miss the moment to say so because you feel afraid of saying something stupid. Then, later on, as the pack consolidates, you feel uncomfortable making jokes, or trying to express your interest in something, because to do so seems like something out of the blue, and also, since you are not integrated into the group, you don't have the guarantee that one of your allies will laugh, or attempt to make you feel more comfortable. If you do say something and receive no reaction, or a negative one, then you are more likely to be even more afraid to speak on the next occasion, and to feel you will be judged on a singular misjudged comment, than if you were already a part of the group. It is a self-perpetuating fear, really. I've been told before that I can come across as aloof or snobby, but I can guarantee that in all those situations it is because I just don't know what to say, and have scared myself into a paralysed silence.

Of course, others, especially the women, I think just saw that I was little shy, and perhaps came from a slightly different background to their own, and worked hard to help me feel comfortable and integrate me into the group.

Even so, a lot of the time it felt like I was just gritting my teeth and sticking it out. In particular, I didn't enjoy the challenges, which are 'fun' competitions that you complete with your partner at intervals throughout the show. Most people love the challenges, they bring a welcome break from the everyday monotony of the villa. I know the villa looks lovely, and it is essentially a holiday, but without books, TV, music or any form of entertainment it gets boring quite quickly and the days do start to merge into one. It's part of the reason everyone ends up talking so much about any drama that is happening – there is literally nothing else to do!

Anyway, this meant that often the challenges were met with a lot of enthusiasm, but I absolutely hated them. From the first slow-mo run out of the villa, down to the deck that was used as the site of all the challenges that took place during the show, I hated it. Do not get me wrong, the challenge team work very hard to come up with fun ideas and most people love them, but it is just not my thing and I felt very exposed and very embarrassed, and it made me awkward with whoever my partner was at that time.

The show ran for seven weeks, and a couple of weeks before the end, Jamie, my now boyfriend, joined the cast as one of the 'bombshells'. We got on immediately, although there wasn't long left in the villa. By that time, I had begun to relax and enjoy the experience a bit more, and I think it was clear to the viewers that the women in the villa had formed a good friendship group at this point, and that's actually the main thing I remember from the last few weeks of the show.

The day of the final felt a bit end-of-term. There wasn't any filming in the villa, as the first half of the show that evening would be from the night before, and then the second half is the live final. Instead, you spend the day getting ready in a nearby villa, so that the *Love Island* villa can be prepped. As we were all getting ready, there was a power cut, and we ended up all having to be driven to a nearby hotel to finish getting ready about thirty minutes before we were due to depart for the final. While it did feel like complete madness, I don't really remember any of us feeling particularly nervous. The thing is, by that point, you are almost more excited about the experience of finishing, of having the opportunity to have your phone back and speak to your friends and family, than you are about the final results. I actually don't think many of us, if any, were that concerned about winning. I'll be honest, from my perspective it didn't feel like Jamie and I could win anyway, we had only been together a really short period of time at that point, and although we were looking forward to getting to know each other better in the real world, we definitely weren't rushing things.

We were, of course, really pleased to be runners-up, but again the real sense of excitement that night comes from when the final is over, and one of the crew comes up to you with a little plastic bag containing your phone, and you can finally turn it on and call your family, and actually catch up with what has been going on in the world for the last seven weeks.

To the best of my knowledge (and I have never watched the *Love Island* season I was in) what you saw in the edit was for the most part representative of what happened on the show. If you haven't watched it, I am not doing it justice because it is all light-hearted good fun. It is about people finding romance in the sun, and, of course, the highs and lows of new relationships. As a contestant, it is also about friendship (as well as finding things to do for seven weeks in a villa with no entertainment). I think you would find the way I talk about the experience very different to the light-hearted, happy vibe of the show itself, and probably also to the other contestants' experiences, and that is just because I was shyer and found the social side more challenging. Ultimately though, *Love Island* proved a very good experience for me, and it really helped to bring me out my shell. With nothing to do all day, and forever trapped in a villa with twelve to fifteen other people, I had no choice but to be sociable. It was entirely inescapable, and that's probably what I needed.

That being said, I did find it immensely exposing, most notably to myself. I had no understanding of my level of insecurity or the reasons behind it. I believed that I had dealt with things that had happened in my life as they had arisen, but within the context of the show I was forced to confront the reality that I hadn't, and I was prompted to try to come to terms with those feelings, since they can and do taint future relationships. *Love Island* gave me structure when I was in chaos, clarity when I was confused.

One of the most talked-about moments from my time on *Love Island* was a debate I had with Jonny about feminism. It was a disagreement that left me visibly upset and after I left the villa at the end of the show, although I received many messages of support on social media, I also saw the many, many messages that mocked my reaction. I understood it in a way, feminism is not often top of everyone's list when looking at romantic compatibility. I know that I became upset a lot during *Love Island* and this shaped people's response to me, but it was the criticism of this moment of misery that hurt me the most. I think it probably brought up some of the frustration I had been feeling in the years previously at not being able to articulate to my friends and family why certain causes had suddenly taken on so much more importance to me, without coming across as a 'bore' or as caring too much about things that didn't affect me.

A part of me doesn't even want to write of this here, because I still feel that very real fear of explaining it and of people not understanding where this frustration at others being treated unfairly comes from. Nor is it only women that I support in being treated equally – it is everyone. It is part of the issue I have with the horrendous way some people view the 'us' and 'them' side of the refugee crisis. I went to places where the LGBTQ(+) community were treated abominably. Similarly, there were instances where people with mental health issues were treated awfully – in one place, as we drove through a village, my driver told me a woman there had seemingly gone mad. She hadn't been bitten by a dog, so they didn't think it was rabies. Instead, they believed she had been bitten by a vampire, whereupon the villagers locked her in an outhouse until eventually she starved to death.

To be honest, whether people thought I was too vulnerable or not, the one thing I still struggle to get on board with is the attitude that you are helping someone build up a thick skin by tearing them down. I know that many people believe that in some way it's 'tough love', and contributing to strengthening that person's overall character, but I actually don't see it as being constructive in any way. I think that that attitude is far more to do with breaking someone down so that you can build them back up the way you want them to be. Often this is in a way that fits them neatly into your understanding of the world. So often we are able to look back at difficult points in our lives and recognise that they helped to make us stronger, but that should be your own judgement to make. It is not for someone else to elect to speak to someone in a humiliating and derogatory fashion in order to 'strengthen them'. It doesn't help people to engage in constructive dialogue, and it sets a precedent that somehow *your* comment is more important than the other person's feelings about it.

I don't believe that you teach people what the 'real world' will be like by abusing or denigrating them. I think you are subduing the world to your own poor standards of communication, while teaching a new generation that it is somehow acceptable to speak to people in a particular way to get them to toughen up. I think that's a real shame, because there is so much strength to be had in not having a thick skin, in being affected by and emotionally invested in people and places and so much else besides.

I think there is definitely a general assumption that if you appear on a programme like *Love Island*, you must be 100 per cent confident in absolutely everything: your looks, your personality, your sense of humour. I often think that this is why people feel comfortable writing abusive comments online to and about those who feature on the show. The reality is very different, however. *Love Island* casts people with interesting back stories, which will often mean that they have experienced significant heartbreak, which in turn takes its toll on confidence or self-esteem. Or people are cast who do talk up the way they view themselves, portraying themselves as full of immutable confidence. Yet the exposing nature of the show often unpicks the fabric of their confidence, and more often than not, identifies the insecurities and misgivings behind the false mask of arrogance. I feel that some people may even augment this behaviour on joining *Love Island*, but, I don't truly believe that anyone knows what they have signed up for and whether they will be able to handle it. You can prepare yourself as best you can, you can surround yourself with people who support and comfort you when you need it. But as with anything you sign up for, you just don't know what it will be like until you are further down the road.

Many broad-brushstroke criticisms have been applied to Love Islanders, one of the most widespread being our stupidity. I found that particularly frustrating. It is very dangerous to characterise a group of people as stupid. Firstly, to label a collective is nearly always ill-informed; it's a reductive way to group people together in a way that the labeller understands. Even if it is intended as a compliment, it is rarely reflective of reality. It is an example of a divisive rhetoric used to create or strengthen an idea of 'us' and 'them'.

Often, I felt these comments were strongly linked to a narrow-minded view of what 'type' of intelligence should be valued, a view that venerates a traditional, old-fashioned intellect at the expense of a more diverse and, in my opinion, often more relevant intelligence. Maligning the latter results in many people being disregarded. To me, this demonstrates a fear of those who do not conform to the traditional system, and so instead the system seeks to dismiss and undermine their abilities. Very often I felt that the individuals who made comments about Love Islanders' stupidity also disregarded their own privilege and educational opportunities, and the power to which that often translates in our society. I feel that whenever a person who has such power, especially those with huge online followings, decides to comment on the intelligence of others, they should consider strongly whether it is necessary, because it often comes at great cost to people's self-esteem, not just those within the group being targeted, but also any who feel they can identify with that group.

There was, however, also a part of me that felt that the reason Love Islanders have been smeared with this idea of a lack of intelligence is because it has been conflated with incidental fame. To an extent, the imposter syndrome I felt post-*Love Island* was because I think that type of incidental fame did feel fraudulent to me. I have always wanted to build something from the hard work I put in, yet everything I had done in the years previously seemed to amount to little, and while I found *Love Island* emotionally challenging, it wasn't hard work. Yet the last seven weeks seemingly amounted to so much more because of the incidental fame that came with them.

I have often been quoted as saying that *Love Island* scared me more than explosive ordnance disposal and that is a statement I stand by. But in both cases I felt like an imposter. The way in which we revere people leads us to believe that it is wholly impossible for us to be like them, and this simply isn't the case. In fact, it is far more likely that they too sit on the sofa in their underwear drinking wine out of the bottle and watching *Real Housewives*, and that they too, pull their dirty tights back out of the laundry basket on a Monday morning. The idea that we are flawed is something we are programmed to believe is, firstly, a weakness and, secondly, a weakness from which only we suffer.

Actually, being an imposter, and pushing ourselves to enter into realms where we do not belong, can be very advantageous. By being brave enough to travel into uncharted territory, it is often the quickest way to find the answers which, in the end, may turn you from imposter to genuine article. It can be what gives you the courage to go for a promotion at work, or to embark on a new career. It is what allowed me to head off to Cambodia, and to every subsequent country I worked in, and I really hope that as much as I may have started out as an imposter, I worked as hard as I could to become a valuable part of a world where I may not have initially belonged.

Yet as soon as I find acceptance, as soon as people tell me I am good at something or that I'm on the right track, that's when I feel most under scrutiny, and find it hardest to perform. It is almost as if whenever I am given an ideal to live up to, that is when I struggle the most, but amid discomfort and confusion, in times when the work seems insurmountable, I am able to mobilise, to keep moving forward and find myself inspired to progress. In comfort I find it harder to move forward. Perhaps I need that friction. I often think of this when I look back to *Love Island* in 2017. In truth, all the obvious comforts were there, but emotionally I felt overwhelmed 99 per cent of the time. In every respect it was a time that should have been the easiest of my life; it was about having fun in a sun-drenched villa and not taking life too seriously. Everything I needed was there, but still I found it distinctly uncomfortable throughout.

A large part of that discomfort stems from my long-held belief that others don't feel the same sense of inadequacy that I do. I suppose that's the explanation – none of us is able to feel the imposter syndrome of those around us. In fact, we are frequently unable even to talk about it. I certainly think there is still a 'fake it till you make it' attitude with which people feel more comfortable. How often do we put our faith in people who seem to know what they are doing? Because we do, they tend to thrive even when a more measured approach might be more useful.

When working in EOD, I was often judged on my gender and young age, and at times struggled to be taken seriously because of them. I have mentioned before that once, after arriving in Yerevan with a male colleague, we couldn't find our driver – it turned out he had been there all along, but he hadn't come over because he was expecting two men. A lot of the time I felt vulnerable, or new and nervous, although I tried to put on a brave face to ensure I could slip seamlessly into a new team. Then, on *Love Island* later, I was initially judged for not being the right fit. People questioned why I was on the show – I was too serious, and not what they expected.

One interesting aspect of views on social media about people in reality TV, is the difference between someone you thought you knew intimately through watching them on your screen, compared with the version of themselves they portray online. Neither can truly encapsulate the truth. To be honest, I don't think this is only true of Love Islanders, it's just that reality TV provides an interesting intersection between the two. Social media is always the edited version of ourselves that we wish to project, and this is true of anyone using the platform. I think if we look at our friends who we know intimately, there is so much more to their lives than what they put online, and, therefore, so much more to them than their Instagram page.

Equally, although reality TV is in some ways very real, exposing love, and life, jealousy, and all the characteristics of humanity, it is also in a way unreal. Twenty-four hours are neatly edited down into a one-hour television show, with a voiceover making it accessible and entertaining to an audience. This is neither a good nor a bad thing – it is just how this kind of television works. After all, the world functions in this way, especially now that it is a much more bite-sized world because of the way we read news. Basically, we turn complex events into digestible chunks, and in doing so, we often end up with a simplified view of the people involved. Sometimes, we use that interpretation to inform how we expect them to behave.

This is no criticism – it is just a reflection on how well people think they know you, and how willing they are to criticise you when either meeting you in person, or following you online, doesn't match up to what they expected. When I first came out of *Love Island* I was frequently told by people who followed me online that I needed to post more, that I should be doing more Instagram stories. That I owed it to the people who had watched me, and especially to those who had voted for me. (Please don't think that I am anything other than extremely grateful to every person who supported me.) What I found difficult was that all the things that weren't very 'me' were the things I was being asked to do on social media, by an audience who now felt they had a right of access to my private life. Equally, on countless occasions I was told that material I had posted wasn't what they expected to see of me. People would send me messages saying that I had disappointed them, and I would feel immense guilt.

It happened in the real world, too. I would be out with friends and having a drink, and people would come over and tell me they never expected it of me. From glasses of ice-cold rosé to Jägerbombs, I cannot tell you how many drinks have been spoilt by a stranger's opinion. I remember meeting someone outside a corner shop one night, when Jamie and I were picking up sweets and crisps, and probably some wine or beer. A small group of guys, probably in their early twenties, recognised us. Actually, they recognised Jamie first, and then one turned to me, turned back to Jamie and said 'That's not the girl you met on *Love Island*,' to which he said, 'Yes, that's Cam.' I was laughing a little – at this time I changed my hairstyle often, and actually I am also frequently told that I don't really look the same in person as I do on camera. Often this is to do with height more than anything else (I am 5 foot 3 on a good day, but seem to look taller on camera). Anyway, the young man turned to me again and, looking straight at me, said, 'No, it's not you.' So I replied, 'Yes, it is me,' at which he said, 'Ah, it must be because you've lost weight, you were much chunkier then.' I said, 'No, I am exactly the same weight,' to which he said 'No, you were definitely much chunkier.' He had been drinking so I didn't really blame him for his frankness, but it is a very strange feeling to be told that even your physical characteristics don't match what someone was expecting.

I was initially very hurt, and I couldn't quite pinpoint why. It should have made little difference to me what he thought, especially as it was something I knew wasn't accurate. But I think it highlighted something that I had previously grappled with, and struggled to understand, when comments were aimed more at my personality traits than my physical ones, namely, how accusatory it often felt people were being when their perception from the TV didn't match the person in real life. In fact, it made me feel that I was the imposter, while they wanted the straightforward Camilla that was familiar to them, and not the complicated one that I actually am.

Over the last few years, our series of *Love Island* has made its way on to other platforms to reach audiences in other countries, and so fairly regularly I would receive messages from people who were only now watching it, telling me what I did right and what I did wrong. That's one of the most interesting aspects of reality TV, seeing that moment in time is captured for ever. That version of you exists for someone to judge at any time. Yet it doesn't take very long for that person you were to feel quite alien to you. I look back and I can't really think the way I thought then. There are many things I don't like about myself (not least the spidery eyelashes), but for a short period of time that woman existed, and now in some format she will exist for ever. I don't regret appearing on *Love Island*, and it would be unfair for me to say that, given what it has helped me through, particularly on a personal level. But I don't recognise the woman who had the guts to go on it, and I couldn't do it now. I don't think that makes me weaker than I was then, I think it makes me different. My priorities have changed, my understanding of my own mental health has changed, my goals have changed.

I have a mild obsession with watching commencement addresses on YouTube. There is one that was given by the late American journalist, writer and filmmaker Nora Ephron, in 1996, in which she talks about a game she would play with her friends when they were waiting for food in restaurants. Each would write down five things to describe themselves. After graduating from college Ephron writes 'ambitious, daughter, Wellesley graduate, Democrat, single'. Ten years later, none of those featured on her list; instead, she was 'journalist, feminist, New Yorker, divorced, funny'. She then goes on to say that on that day none of those descriptions featured on her list. Now she was 'writer, director, mother, sister, happy'. We are not immutable, but that version of us that is trapped in reality TV has been given a permanence that belies the truth of the woman behind it. She will not be allowed to grow with you.

We have seen an interesting phenomenon in the last decade, that when children are asked what they want to be they often say 'famous', without thought as to what they might be famous for. I hasten to add that I believe some of these studies to have been scientifically flawed, but what is interesting is the candour of the children who do answer that they wish to be famous, which is not so easily seen in adults who may find themselves attracted to the idea of fame, but not wish to admit it, even to themselves. Fame does seem to provide an easy answer to questions of self-confidence and identity; there are hundreds, thousands, and for some, millions of other people who will bolster those for you.

If I'm completely honest, I think for a time fame did seem to offer a shortcut to happiness. I can't quite pinpoint where this perception came from, but it was certainly something I had picked up over the years, perhaps initially from TV and magazines, and more recently from social media platforms. I don't think I was ever convinced reality TV or even fame itself were really the right thing for me, but I did have a belief that famous people were happy, and that fame itself provided some protection from life's difficulties. When I first came out of *Love Island*, I wouldn't say I got carried away, but I had a false sense of security in the idea that now I would be happy. This didn't last more than a few days, but for a fleeting moment, the promise of gold at the end of the rainbow seemed entirely true. I now recognise the darker side of fame, not just for the 'famous' but also the non-famous. It tells people that their lives are not enough, that they could be happier, that things could be better, but that promise is always just out of reach.

Truly, I think fame comes at a cost for everyone. So while I can't regret *Love Island*, for so many reasons, I can look back now and realise the consequences of the trappings of fame. Not just for me individually, but also for a generation of younger people, the audience who saw only the good side of that experience. Who saw the sunshine, and the laughter, a sparkling blue pool and colourful bikinis. I worry now, in a way that I could not have understood going into *Love Island*, that I have perpetuated an ideal of fame, that I am complicit in selling the idea that fame holds the easiest of answers.

I don't think it's fair to say my life has been harder because of *Love Island*. Life can be hard, and there are ups and downs, no matter where you end up. What I think is a universal truth, though, is that what we are told will bring us joy and happiness is not always the answer it may appear to be. So, keep holding on to things that do bring you comfort when you need it, be they the folded-down corners of your favourite book, or your mum's recipe for spaghetti bolognaise, or the sheer glee when you play a perfect round of Articulate. Be conscious that these are not invalid because of what you see celebrated in the public realm as the accepted route to happiness. There are too many people who have walked down that path already, only to report back not only of the tears, terrors and overwhelming disappointment, but that happiness was not to be found.

Chapter 8

Rush Hour

———

I didn't have a permanent address after I left *Love Island*. The finalists had a couple of days in an hotel after the show finished, and I wasn't sure what to do after that. In the end, I stayed in London with various kind friends over the coming weeks. One lent me her flat in Notting Hill for two weeks while she was away on holiday, and then I stayed on bedroom floors or sofas. I hadn't had much money before I went in to *Love Island*, and when I came out, I had about enough to get some warmer clothes (I only had the wardrobe of clothes from the villa), and for general expenses.

In the first few days, I was asked if I would do a photoshoot with *Grazia* that ITV had arranged. It was my second ever shoot (the first being the *Love Island* publicity day), so Lewis, the casting producer of the show, and Justin, the publicity manager, joined me. I turned up early to a studio with no makeup on, and I don't think the team there initially recognised me. Eventually, the woman running the shoot came over and was very kind and welcoming. She kept mentioning how small I am, and this was my first taste of how I looked in person not matching up with how I looked on screen. As I have said several times, I am 5 foot 3 inches tall (on a good day), but I seemed to look much taller on camera, for everyone I met in the coming weeks would comment on how much smaller I was in person. I suppose a part of this is because a lot of your actual screen time on *Love Island* is filmed when you are in the Beach Hut, sitting talking directly to the camera, and it is always hard to gauge how tall someone is when you aren't being compared against someone else's stature. Also, I have a theory about why I often look taller or bigger in photos or on camera. It is a theory that Jamie finds hilarious but I remain convinced – it is because of my pea head. I have an absolutely tiny head, disproportionately small for my body, which makes everything else look bigger in comparison.

In the end, I loved the *Grazia* shoot. I looked tired and surprisingly pale given that I had just spent seven weeks in the sun (there was a funny moment in *Love Island* when one of the bombshells first arrived and asked me if I'd been staying out of the sun because everyone was so much more tanned than me). Julie, the makeup artist, was so kind to me, making me look and feel as good as possible. She could tell I was nervous and told me funny stories, and showed me pictures and explained all the products she was using. During *Love Island*, we had had two days out of the seven weeks when we were offered one beauty treatment (this did not included waxing). On the second of these days, I opted for individual lashes, but unfortunately they had ended up very spidery. At the time of the *Grazia* shoot I hadn't had the time to have the remnants removed and replaced, and by then half my own lashes had actually fallen out as a result, but Julie very gently applied temporary infills that fluffed them out. Sitting in that chair, I gradually began to feel more like myself. I never really knew the application of makeup could be like that. I had never had my makeup done for me before, and I'm not the best at doing my own. By the end I looked like me, but so much better, though not just because of the makeup – it was because she made me feel that I deserved to be there, and in turn my face brightened.

I then went over to the stylist, Stephen, terrified that I was going to be confronted with a rail of swimwear. Instead there were simple shirts, a huge turtleneck jumper and the most gorgeous white dress with black ribbon at the collar that did right up to my neck. Having only ever done the press shoot for *Love Island*, I was relieved not to see a row of bikinis. These clothes felt much more my style.

I had expected the shoot to be an awful experience for me. I don't like having my photograph taken, and I'm not good at relaxing in the company of strangers. After the photographer had shot the first round of photos, they showed me some of them on a big screen, and I was pleasantly surprised – people tend to be when they realise what it is like to be photographed with their hair and makeup professionally done, proper styling, great lighting, and a talented photographer and creative team.

ITV were well aware that it was likely I would be unsure what to do in the weeks immediately following *Love Island*. When you first come out, you do find yourself bombarded with media requests, as well as several DMs about Instagram product promotion. I was at a complete loss of how to deal with it all and needed someone to guide me through it. They had kindly kept a list of all the agents who had expressed an interest in speaking to me while I was in the show. Meanwhile, my friends who had looked after my Instagram account had kept an amazing Word document listing all the different people who had tried to contact me whilst I was in the villa. (My Instagram account has never been as well managed as it was by them, and for a long time I wanted to hand responsibility for it back to them.) They were the ones who had actually had to respond to the rapid growth in the number of followers, and to field comments from every quarter. They had to make decisions about what content to share, as well as about how to deal with negative comments and messages. It was essentially a full-time job, and they executed it perfectly. They are the main reason why I started mostly on the right track with Instagram, and in those early days after leaving the villa, it was to them that I would send photos before I posted them online, to check what they thought.

After the *Grazia* shoot, Lewis, Justin and I went back to the ITV offices where Justin and the *Love Island* publicity team had kindly organised half-hour meetings with about ten or eleven different agencies in their meeting room. They handed me a list of the agencies and the representatives from each that we would be meeting. It took me about four of these meetings to actually understand what was going on: they were pitching to me. They wanted me as their client. I don't really know anyone directly in the 'showbiz' world, but I do have a couple of close friends who have tried to break into acting, directing, screen writing, and I knew from them how fiercely competitive and tricky it was. It felt very odd and back-to-front for these agencies to be pitching to me. The reality was that although we had been briefed the night the show ended it had drastically increased in viewership, I hadn't at that stage fully understood its popularity. I also didn't really have any clear idea of the world of social media influencers, and so I wasn't entirely aware of the value that brands may (or may not) have seen in me as a contributor to the show.

There were some extremely nice people I met in those meetings, the best being the three who asked me what I was looking to achieve, whether I was interested in fashion, beauty or perhaps writing. I had no idea whom to pick, and so Justin and Lewis told me that almost always the best thing to do is to set up a second meeting at the agency's office, and to pick the person with whom I felt I could go for a drink! Looking back, this was great advice. You spend so much time speaking to your agent, that on some days, when you are working on things at home, they will be the main person you talk to on the phone. They have to get what you're about, and be able to tell you the truth about the potential risks of various jobs. You need to feel that they're on your side, but not in an exploitative way. I actually only went for one follow-up interview with my favourite from among the people I had met on the first day and after that, I was absolutely sure that I hoped to sign with John Noel Management, who have looked after me ever since.

It took a couple of weeks to go through the process of the second meeting and getting the contract in place and signed. At this point, I still didn't have any money, and I hadn't made any yet, either. I was being invited to a lot of events, but I just didn't have the money to go. I had spent the last bit of cash I had in the bank on two tickets to Greece for me and Jamie to go and work with Indigo Volunteers. At this point, we didn't know exactly what to expect we would be doing, as we were to join a range of projects in different camps over the few days, and just lend a hand where necessary. This was mainly assisting with: food preparation and distributions, providing care in safe spaces for women, and offering activities and lessons for children. I began to feel myself again as soon as we packed up my big North Face bag and set off to the airport. We had hoped to grab a beer before boarding our flight, but it was the beginning of August and the airport was absolutely crammed with people.

It was probably the most that we have ever been recognised. We literally couldn't go two feet without being stopped for a photo. In the end, we separated and ran to the gate to get there in time without being stopped. We boarded a completely packed plane, and squashed ourselves into the window seats and ate the sandwiches Jamie had managed to pick up from Pret à Manger as he ran past. We had one change in Munich, and then a final flight on to Thessaloniki, the largest city in Macedonia, in northern Greece. There we were met by Indigo's founder and CEO, Holly Penalver, whom I also knew a little from university. She drove us back to the Indigo flat in the city. It was coming up for 11 p.m. and she briefed us during the journey so that we would be ready to go in the morning.

Over the next week, we visited various projects including A Drop in the Ocean, Soul Food Kitchen, InterVolve Volunteers and Lifting Hands for which Indigo helps to match volunteers. I think we both breathed a sigh of relief as we landed in Greece, and our anonymity was restored. Not only did we feel practical and useful, but I no longer felt under scrutiny. Indigo was formed to counter the exploitative practices of for-profit volunteering agencies, who look to make money from well-meaning people who wish to volunteer. Often people won't know the best avenue to volunteer, or will be unable to find the correct project where their skills will be most useful. That is where Indigo comes in to match volunteers with grassroots projects that most need their help.

There is a great deal of bureaucracy within the charity sector, partly due to grant reporting – how you explain how the projects will be implemented to the person or organisation providing the money – and partly due to internal due diligence in terms of ensuring the correct procedures are in place to safeguard both the charity, its finances and employees, as well as the beneficiaries of the charity's work. Much of it is extremely necessary (some is not), but sometimes it means that larger charities are unable to mobilise as quickly as smaller operations to redirect funds to complete the activities that are needed the most, without going through extensive and time-consuming reporting procedures and applications to governing bodies.

As a result, there is undoubtedly a place for both. In order for any small charity to be effective, it needs to be able to use funds as efficiently as possible. However, many of these smaller grassroots charities are operating on a shoestring, and don't have the staff, time or money to recruit their own volunteers, which is why Indigo's work to provide a match-making service, is so valuable.

We spent our days in Greece with these smaller charities. On the final day, we joined Lifting Hands, an international charity providing humanitarian aid to refugees, in Serres. The Greek authorities do not allow organisations to work within the camp, so Lifting Hands had set up in a park, about a hundred metres away. Here they taught classes to the Yazidi children and teenagers who were staying in Serres camp.

The story of what happened to the Yazidis, an ancient ethnic and religious minority indigenous to Iraq, Syria and Turkey, is truly awful. Following the withdrawal of the Peshmerga, the Kurdish military forces, from Sinjar in northern Iraq in 2014, ISIL began to attack the now unprotected Yazidi community, believing them to be 'devil-worshippers'. They started to kill men, and reportedly buried women and children alive. These killings began to gain momentum, until the Yazidi population were given an ultimatum by ISIL – either convert to Islam or be killed or held as slaves. In Kocho village, an elder refused, whereupon the men were rounded up into trucks. They were told they were being taken to Sinjar, but in fact were shot. Thousands of women and children were abducted, many to be used as sex slaves. Other Yazidi villages were set on fire, and as terror spread through the population, those who could, fled to the Sinjar Mountains. There they were surrounded, and large numbers of them succumbed to exposure and dehydration; many were children.

The Yazidi women and girls who were abducted as sex slaves were taken to ISIL markets. They were examined to discover whether they were virgins or pregnant; often those who were pregnant were given forced abortions. Nadia Murad, now a human-rights campaigner who was one of those kidnapped from Sinjar, has given a first-hand account of the market, describing the militants who walked around surveying the screaming, begging women and girls, and selected their victims.

Nadia's account is not only a tale of phenomenal resilience, but she also showed great courage in coming forward to tell a story knowing that her life would be for ever changed in the process. Often those who talk about traumatic experiences do so to bring their persecutors to justice. They may or may not find the process cathartic, but what is certain is that no matter how far their lives move away from the event, that moment is still trapped in time, multiplied by thousands as their narrative is disseminated across media platforms, and that is overwhelming for any person. Nadia's sacrifice in talking about her ordeal is immense, for there is always a painful reminder for her just within her sight, something that is inescapable. Other Yazidi women who obtained their freedom have now made their way to countries such as Germany, only to encounter their captors, now refugees themselves, in the street.

It is estimated that 3,000 Yazidi women and children are still enslaved by Islamic State. It is a staggering number, and in such a close-knit community, pretty much without exception, the refugees in Serres camp would either be the family or friends of those still missing to this day. They don't know exactly where they are, or what torment they are suffering, but they do know that it is highly likely they are being subjected to sexual torture, to beatings, to any number of unthinkable cruelties. In 2016, a horrific story emerged that nineteen of the Yazidi women and girls who had been taken, had refused to be sex slaves, and as punishment were placed in iron cages and burned to death with hundreds of people watching.

The last class we attended with Lifting Hands was an English lesson for girls ranging from fourteen to seventeen years old. I knew the story of the Yazidi genocide. I knew that these girls would have friends or family who had been taken, going through unimaginable suffering – there was absolutely no denying this. I can't describe how many emotions boiled up inside me at that moment. I was so grateful that these girls hadn't been taken, and so desperately sad for those who had, and were now enduring such horrific torture. The women and girls who might never make it home, and if they did would be so horrendously damaged by their ordeal. And I was so moved by the beautiful, smart, funny, ambitious girls who sat in front of me, wise beyond their years. It is hard for me not to talk about them as young women, because they were so grown-up in the way they spoke.

The final part of the lesson was learning words about careers and professions, and each in turn said what she would like to be when she grew up. They talked about becoming doctors, lawyers and journalists, and every single one, when they explained the reasons for their choice, spoke about how they wanted to help people. Some talked about the time when they were trapped in the mountains and they realised that no one was coming to rescue them, and said they didn't want others ever to feel alone as they had. They were children whose childhoods had been stolen from them. It was they who found the strength to grow in the darkness, to make their own light and offer it to the world.

Something in the stories of these girls makes me wonder about the very tenets of masculinity and femininity as they have been stereotyped and understood. I am not saying that masculinity or femininity are wholly bad or wholly good, but I do find it difficult to accept that the attributes that have been classed as female traits – empathy, care and vulnerability – are often seen as weak, while those seen as male traits – physical strength, power, and an ability to detach from emotions – are seen as strong.

To me, it is exactly those female traits that gave these girls the strength it must have taken to find a way to keep moving forward, despite their pain. In contrast, the very things the perpetrators believed made them strong – their ability to fight to kill and to take exactly what they wanted, at terrible cost to the people around them – actually made them weak.

I think that our understanding of strength and what it equates to, particularly when distorted to fit into patriarchal structures, means that we lose sight of the value of empathy and compassion, and how immensely strong those qualities are. I am certain that had these young women gone on to live the lives they deserved – had they grown up and got jobs, had they mothered children, had they led the normal lives they were meant to – very few other people would have seen the immensity of strength in that. Perhaps, then, the compassion, empathy and thoughtfulness which, as a result of their terrible experiences, meant that they all aspired to professions in which they could help others, would not have been so recognisable as an exhibition of strength, and rather would have been seen as traits that have traditionally been typecast as 'weaker'.

When we got back, after a couple of weeks, I got a job with LookFantastic, the online cosmetics company, as part of their Christmas advertisement. While this was being filmed, a story appeared that I had signed a £500,000 contract to appear in the advert. I think it started in the *Sun*, and was then picked up by several other media outlets. To this day, I don't know where the story came from; maybe the figure was for the overall budget that had been discussed at some point. I have no idea. But I had a lot of messages sent to me on Instagram, telling me how to spend that £500,000 (which of course never existed). They told me that I needed to wear more expensive clothes, that I should be using a stylist because I clearly couldn't put outfits together myself, that my makeup looked cheap. Or they told me off for not announcing that I had given a large lump sum away, adding that I must have just been pretending to be a nice person if I was going to accept half a million pounds for myself and not give any of it to anyone.

The fee was great (though in fact a long way from six figures), but obviously it was nothing like what was being reported. A percentage of that goes to your agent, and I had also borrowed money in the interim so I had people to pay back, as well as clear other debts and bills from before *Love Island*. I wasn't paid that fee for a few months, either, and within that time I didn't have any income, but I was still being invited to events, so I was borrowing money for clothes, and also for living expenses.

I usually bought all the dresses I wore back then myself, as I was rarely lent anything, and often I was just picking what I could afford at the time. I did my own hair and makeup. Nothing could have prepared me for the scrutiny you receive, both in the media and online, over how you look and what you wear, and I took a lot of the criticism very much to heart. I still didn't have a permanent place to live in London, so often I was getting ready in friends' bedrooms – and once in the toilet at Jamie's gym! I was constantly living out of suitcases and never had what I needed with me, and felt very under pressure to look a certain way, when I didn't really have the means to do so. I simply didn't have that money, but comments about the way I looked still hurt. They still hurt now, if I'm honest, for we commit these judgements to heart. How often do we recall the admonishing voice of someone from school whom we haven't seen for decades? It was that feeling but multiplied, and the little confidence I had started to build up in *Love Island* started to crumble away.

I remember once, I met a close friend for a drink at Liverpool Street station as our different journeys coincided there, and she filmed me eating some nachos. At the time, I was carrying pretty much everything I needed with me, because I was going between friends' sofas in London and visiting Jamie's parents' place in Essex. I had travelled on the tube to Liverpool Street with all my stuff at rush hour and was hot, bothered, and very dishevelled. My arm ached from carrying too many tote bags (my backpack was in Scotland), and there were deep red indents in my shoulder. My friend put up a little Instagram story of me eating nachos and laughing, and I reshared it on my own Instagram story. I started receiving messages: 'Why are you so dishevelled?', 'You shouldn't go out looking messy like that,' 'Such a shame that you don't look after yourself,' 'You've got to make more of an effort now'.

Naturally, these messages were all from strangers. Some of them went on to be prolific trollers. Some were more well-meaning, a more genuine attempt to tell me to up my game, and in a way that felt more hurtful. I think this unasked-for commentary had more influence than I realised at the time. I definitely did start to worry about how I looked – even when I was just walking to the shops, I would worry about being recognised. I would panic when I saw a horrible photograph of me in the media, because I knew that inevitably someone would send me a message on Instagram with a comment about it. There would be comments like 'Why do you look so weird in this photo?' The worst ones always open with 'Sorry to tell you this but...'. Gratuitous remarks like 'Sorry to tell you this but you just aren't that attractive'; 'Sorry to tell you this but you're just another face in the crowd'. I'm not going to lie, I don't think that input was needed at all, so if you are that sorry to tell me – don't tell me!

I have never been one of those people who is good at looking 'polished' or 'done', and the amount of time I began to spend worrying about how I looked, or lamenting ill-chosen outfits, was ridiculous. I don't think it's wrong to be interested in clothes or makeup; actually I think it's perfectly reasonable to be an informed individual working on things you believe in, and at the same time have a very real passion for mascara. The two are not mutually exclusive. But I think at this point in my life, the balance I had previously struck between the two shifted too much in the wrong direction. I felt very dissatisfied, and I think a large part of that came from adjusting to a new way of working as I became more of an ambassador for certain causes and no longer had my own boots on the ground, while at the same time caring way too much about what people said about how I looked.

It started to make me feel that I didn't deserve to have appeared on *Love Island* in the first place because I couldn't keep up. It reminded me of being at school and never having the latest thing – the yoyo with flashing lights, the Tamagotchi with ten different animal settings, the purple lava lamp – the feeling of always being one step behind the crowd. I started to spend far too much money on clothing, and with each paycheque, would purchase far more than I could afford or needed. Things that I would once have worn a hundred times over, I would buy and wear once. If someone posted a negative comment, I wouldn't wear that item again. If people liked what I had worn, I can't deny that I would be pleased, but I would rarely repeat the outfit because it had already been seen.

I started to realise that not only was this not good for me, it just wasn't a responsible way to be shopping. I did not need this quantity of clothes. To be honest, on a day-to-day basis, I still mainly wore the same things over and over, I didn't really enjoy the process of putting together outfits, and spending thirty minutes each morning trying to plan what to wear didn't appeal to me. I had a few favourites that I knew to be comfortable, and repeated them like a uniform. When I knew I'd be seen, however, and, worse, perhaps photographed, then I would stress myself out, and try to plan a whole new outfit. It didn't change anything for me, there was no satisfaction to be had from it. I still felt as though I couldn't keep up, and I knew that the relentless shopping was bad for me financially, and also that the world of fast fashion had potentially bigger implications of which I did not want to be a part. I remembered being happier when I had four HALO T-shirts and two pairs of khaki trousers. Some people love fashion, and are good at it. Some people have a gift for putting together clothes and colours (my mum is one of them). I am not. I find it stressful. I genuinely appreciate it as a skill in other people, I think it is a true talent. That said, however, what I wear is to my mind one of the least interesting things about me, because of my lack of interest and skill in it.

The other part of it that made and still makes me uncomfortable is the idea that we always need to have the latest thing – I don't believe that the concept that happiness is constantly just out of reach, and with the next purchase you just might be able to achieve it, is good for anyone's mentality. There is giving people options, and then there is making people feel inadequate so that they always need more, or believe they do. Often this happens at the expense of both the environment, and the people within the manufacturing chain. I'm not saying that people shouldn't be allowed to dress nicely if they like to. How we dress and present ourselves is often an important part of self-expression. But encouraging people to feel inadequate and unhappy in order to sell clothes (or any of countless other items) is not something I feel comfortable with at all. It suggests there is an external quick fix for internal struggles. What I was actually struggling with at that time was my sense of identity and self-worth. Rather than dealing with that, it was easier to believe that if I managed to put together the right outfit for the right event, the subsequent praise would make me feel confident.

I had started taking regular CBT (cognitive behavioural therapy) sessions over Skype, and, feeling drained, exhausted and mixed up after each session, I would comfort myself by browsing the ASOS website and buying something (usually a jumpsuit), knowing that within twenty-four hours I would be able to wear my new outfit and would feel 'myself' again.

Not the Type

I gave up CBT after spending many hours after the sessions in frustrated tears that I couldn't seem to explain the life I had had with HALO, or the life I had now. To be fair, I've never been a good communicator, but I also hadn't taken into account that different therapists have different areas of specialisation. The therapist I was seeing had come highly recommended by someone else, and has worked wonders with others, but I needed to be able to communicate, over Skype, about complex and distressing events that needed a lot of context that she didn't have. I probably should have looked to identify someone with particular experience in humanitarian work, and/or someone with experience of being in the public eye. I got very little out of the sessions because I couldn't open up, and I found the whole process of explanation draining. One day, I told her that I just couldn't continue, and she left the door open for me to go back and start again. She also said that she hoped I would do CBT again at some point, even if it wasn't with her.

Looking back now, I think I was able to put on a face that made it seem that I was fine. When I first came out of *Love Island*, I was just so relieved to feel more myself, and for the most part, I stayed away from things I would find too overwhelming, while I was brilliantly looked after by my management, who found exactly the right balance from the start. But, I still struggled to understand how to claim my place in this new version of life, and felt I was constantly being buffeted this way and that with very little direction of my own, partly as a result of putting too much stock in the online commentary.

Rush Hour

It is only on looking back now that I realise that I used a lot of temporary fixes to try to patch over long-term problems, chiefly that I really didn't know what I actually wanted to do next. My life was changing very quickly, and there was always another thing I could focus on. There was always another event, or another Instagram post. I let all those daily distractions absorb me so that the hours and the days would slip away unnoticed, and so that I didn't have to confront the fact that I really had no idea what the future would hold. I think in doing so, I let the external chaos become internal turmoil, and became less sure of myself and who I am, and more susceptible to being emotionally affected by the running commentary online.

Chapter 9

Social Media

___

After *Love Island*, many people asked me how I coped with the constant scrutiny that comes with the type of fame cultivated by participating in a reality TV show. 'How does it feel to always be watched?' people asked, 'to be consistently judged?' 'What's it like having over a million Instagram followers?' Really, though, I have spent my whole life feeling like the world was watching. I genuinely once read an article about people hiding cameras in toilets, and to this day I still put my hand over any clear location for a camera to be hidden. I think it stems a lot from going to boarding school at ten years old, where your every move is marked by your peers. Or perhaps it is sheer ego. Whatever it is, my whole life I have felt that every decision I make is scrutinised and notched up by some invisible judgement board who give me points for every decision, and how it reflects my moral character.

Not the Type

One of the most interesting aspects of the *Love Island* phenomena is the engagement of viewers in debates on social platforms, particular Twitter. In Jamie Bartlett's book *The People vs Tech – How the internet is killing democracy (and how we save it)*, he talks about how 'knowing the things you say are collected and shared ensures a soft but constant self-censorship'. I think this is particularly pertinent for young people. They are growing up in a world where their lives – every mistake, every miscalculated comment – are, to borrow a phrase from *The Social Network*, written in ink.

Without the opportunity to make mistakes, and move on from them, to engage in debate and not have one ill-judged tweet follow them for the rest of their lives, they aren't given the opportunity to develop their skills in exercising moral judgement. And yet, when *Love Island* hit you immediately saw thousands of people engaging online in avid debate. It's a commentary on one of the most important aspects of human life – relationships – and yet perhaps because it is so seemingly innocuous people feel able to voice their opinions, and to produce some hilarious memes!

Equally, there is a downside to the media interest. There is an immediate influx of stories, as well as comments on social media, that when you leave the show, initially you are not equipped to deal with. My first impression was that people couldn't see that you feel exactly the same way they would. A bit frightened and very vulnerable.

This isn't specific to *Love Island*, although the transition to suddenly being in the media spotlight is an abrupt one. People in the public eye for whatever reason, are under scrutiny, and alongside this they are accessible on social media. Actually, this now extends well beyond the media spotlight. Social media is a platform for anyone, and as a result, anyone who uses social media is in a position to be scrutinised. That feedback, whether positive or negative, can feel quite disconcerting, as it offers the contributions of thousands of strangers who don't have a full understanding of your life. Your private world becomes public property, but those who comment only have a small window into that world, a fragment of what makes up the full complexity of your life. As a result, the comments can feel very personal, but at the same time aren't particularly useful because the person delivering them doesn't have all the information. People forget that these are real people's lives. I've watched it over and over again – rape threats, death threats – as if these would ever help to resolve a situation, as if these could do anything other than damage people's health, their sanity, their chance of recovery.

It is almost as though the scrutinisers can't remember feeling that way themselves, whether insecure, or possessed by a sense of self-loathing in the wake of mistakes – which I think is the lowest ebb for so many of us. Your misery can feel like public property, and other people's interpretation of events becomes fact, whether it echoes reality or not. I think that has been one of my biggest takeaways – the sheer capacity for cruelty in the name of a few more clicks on an article, or a few more likes on a photo. The real danger is that you stop seeing yourself the way that most other people see you, and instead do so through this highly negative lens.

It is a dangerous dislocation that isolates you in a headspace that isn't real.

The behaviour of some people on social media reminds me strongly of the famous experiment conducted in the 1960s by Stanley Milgram, a psychologist at Yale University. He was investigating the human tendency towards obedience. One 'naive' subject was placed in a room in which there was equipment on which were controls clearly marked with voltage levels denoting electric shocks that ranged from mild to severe. It was explained to the unwitting subject that the study was to do with learning, and that they were to administer ever-increasing shocks to a person in a second room for every incorrect answer that person gave to a question. Unbeknownst to the subject, the person being shocked was actually an actor, who had a list of responses to the questions, as well as guidelines on when to pound on the wall to simulate pain.

The subjects were being tested on the highest level they would shock the 'learner' at before refusing to continue. Anyone who refused to shock the 'learner' up to the maximum level (marked 'XXX', and classified as 450 volts) was deemed a defiant subject. Of the forty men who participated, only fourteen stopped before that level, with twenty-six continuing up to the maximum strength of shock they could administer. It is worth noting here that a group of Yale seniors with psychology majors had been asked prior to the experiment to predict how many of the subjects would continue until the end, and they had all stated they thought it would be an insignificant minority. In fact, the highest result they got was a likelihood that 3 in 100 would continue administering electric shocks until the end of the experiment.

I first learned about this experiment when I was young, from a documentary, and I distinctly remember being really worried about how I would have reacted, because at that time, I thought I was relatively obedient. Even the subjects who administered shocks right up to the maximum 'were observed to sweat, tremble, stutter, bite their lips, groan, and dig their fingernails into their flesh',[12] but they still continued. Even though we are taught from childhood that causing pain to others is wrong, we are also taught to obey the people we view as legitimate authority figures. In our younger years, we have little choice over who those authority figures will be. They are usually our parents, our family elders, our teachers. Later, we learn about the police, and later still perhaps the government. To have been taught to obey the pervasive voice is often useful, for the most part, you are learning the ways of the world. It has also been conjectured, that a willingness to obey a leader was often advantageous to survival, even when in terms of split second decisions like 'Do I run from this woolly mammoth or not?'

I am easily institutionalised. On *Love Island* we had no sense of time (you aren't allowed watches). We got up when we were told to, we ate when we were told to, we went to bed when we were told to. For some people this was immensely challenging, but I found this the easiest part of adapting to the experience. Because I'm such an overthinker

---

[12] Milgram, S. (1963). Behavioural study of obedience. *Journal of Abnormal and Social Psychology*, 67(4), 371-378

and 'catastrophiser', any kind of choice or decision is fraught with worry for me. At my worst, when I am feeling extremely anxious and my OCD tendencies really kick in, I can convince myself that if I pick the wrong clothes to put on that morning, something terrible will happen to my family that day. So any type of decision being taken out of my hands feels like a release for me.

My brother is exceptionally intelligent, and when we were younger he frequently cast a critical eye over what he considered to be unnecessary or ill-informed rules, and then disregarded them, happy to make his own decisions. I was always malleable, and keen to follow someone else's rules. It was daunting for me on leaving HALO to consider creating a structure for myself. After years of morning parades and uniforms, freedom was a novelty for a mere second before I found it completely overwhelming, and that feeling was echoed when I left *Love Island*. Powerful voices influence me, and my life has been marked and shaped by the persuasive voices I have chosen to listen to. After *Love Island* there was a gap, as that structure was removed, and in part I filled it with the voices I heard online, with the interactions I had on social media that told me what I should be doing.

But as I pause to reflect on the most pervasive voices in my life I am struck by how close we are now to people who don't necessarily know us best, or have our best interests at heart, through social media. I think back to my early twenties and trying to explain to my mum why Facebook was SO important, even though I would come off the computer in tears. My distrust of social media is not necessarily a

Luddite standpoint, it's more the point that online we are now expected to be interpreting information and making decisions that we may not be equipped to make.

I think one of the choices we are given as we get older is who we want to listen to. To an extent, we are still bound to structures that require us to listen to certain people as authority figures, such as our boss, but we also have far greater agency than when we are young. In short, when we become adult, we don't have to listen to our parents anymore, or our teachers, and often we take great joy in the sense of control we now have about who we listen to.

Generation Z, however, are, I think, being asked to make those decisions earlier and earlier because they are exposed to a globalised world through their smartphone screens, which in turn means that they have to start exercising their moral judgement long before I was ever expected to. The people who were so crucial in shaping our worlds (like parents and teachers), start to lose out to a pervasive and persistent online voice that it as a complex as it is contradictory. And in juggling with this, young people have absolutely no margin for error. If they choose to draw a judgement, or even just like a post which suggests where their allegiances lie, that is it, that opinion now exists in the internet, with the permanence of an ink pen that cannot be erased at some later date.

When we need an escape from the realities of life, social media feels like a blessing and a curse. It is the medium of the daydreamers, shaped to look concrete, providing the perfect avenue for escape. In many ways, it has become the dopamine hit needed to get through the day; that moment when we finally sit down on the sofa, and breathe a sigh of relief as we look at our phone and are able to remove ourselves from real life. Yet it makes normal, 'average' life seem utterly unbearable, despite that being the reality for the majority. So much of the real magic of living a normal life is the nuance and the smaller moments, that just cannot fit into a space that demands sensationalism and success in others' eyes, above all. We know the crushing reality that comes with escapism, the hangover after the bottle of wine the night before, the end of a good book as we close the final page and suddenly the characters that had become our best friends have finished the part of the story we are allowed to be a part of. We know what it is like to come back down to earth with a bump, to crash land back in our own reality, only to feel we need another escape.

I actually really loved the initial years of Instagram, and before that YouTube. I had grown up looking at models knowing I would never look like that – as I've said, I'm not tall, and all too often I would purchase clothing that simply wouldn't look the same on me. Then suddenly there were people out there who did look like me. I could follow them on Instagram or YouTube, and see which clothes looked better on them, and know those would actually look better on me too. I was able to make more informed purchases. I bought fewer items I had to return. I could watch people try make-up products, and see if they had the kind of effect I was looking for. I had all the advice I could possibly need, and it felt like it came from people who were similar to who I am, which actually I think many were. I felt included in this world. I felt like I was represented in a way I hadn't when I saw fashion magazines growing up. Yes, I was determined to succeed and to give back, even from that young age, but I was still interested in make-up and magazines.

Since then, it feels as if something has changed in the overall tone of social media. Whilst the 'explore' and 'suggestions' features seem like an added benefit to us, they are often steering us towards our own doubts. How often has someone who you don't want to see appeared in your explore feed? The dizzying world of algorithms and metadata seems to be advantageous, but information we DON'T want to see is equally as compelling – perhaps even more so – than that which we do want to see. Not only that, but it is also extremely advantageous from a commercial viewpoint to ensure that we are feeling a bit inadequate, all the time. Therefore, even if you successfully curate your feed to be positive, and leave you feeling good about yourself (and that is difficult in itself), there is still a high chance you will still be exposed to images or information that may be damaging to you. Although at times we may be unwise in our choices of the people we follow, or the picture we choose to click on, knowing that they are things that will cause us to feel inadequate, we aren't wholly responsible for the toxic information we take in online.

There are also collective trends that appear on media platforms, and are hugely influential in the content that we see a lot of. One of the most pervasive themes, and in my opinion one of the most dangerous, has been to do with health, diet and wellness. Day after day we see clickbait articles about 'celebrities' who have lost weight, with information on how they did so – except often these people have been in no way affiliated with the article. Instead, the person who wrote it often cherry-picks information from other interviews the person has given, using any mention of food they can find. Another fad that has also become increasing prevalent is the insidious wellness-based trends. These have included the ridiculous (perineum sunning), but also more worrying trends such as that of dry fasting. Dry fasting means going for significant periods of time without drinking water, which is exceptionally dangerous. Going without water for extended periods of time is detrimental to a huge number of bodily processes. Yet people were posting images of themselves in bikinis, talking about the benefits of dry fasting. This is an example of a singularly dangerous fad, that has already to some extent taken hold despite being publicly refuted by healthcare professionals and demonstrates the 'telephone' nature of social media, and how myths are perpetuated and begin to look credible as, further along the chain of influence, the questionable origins of such fads become increasingly less visible. There are many, many others, proliferating and multiplying, and these are made ever more relevant and believable, by the diet and wellness led climate online.

The insidious nature of diet myths is not only damaging in terms of the varying dangerous theories that unlicensed individuals are able to promote online, but I can only imagine the sheer level of triggers that people encounter on social media on a daily basis, be that through articles, or individual pages. I suspect, though, that there is a similar difficulty that

I have, which is trigger avoidance. One of the hardest things to do is protect yourself from what you are vulnerable to. For some reason, so many of us have an irrepressible urge to look at things that will hurt us. At the woman whose body type who we can't possibly hope to emulate, at the acquaintance we went to university with who got a lucky break and now lives somewhere far sunnier and more luxurious than us, and, of course, at our exes.

I love seeing content about people's real lives, I find it fascinating, but having that forum for comparison is a dangerous one. We are expected to be grown up enough to manage our natural emotions of jealousy and envy. We are meant to have learnt how to embrace being happy for someone else, without feeling any dubiousness at the satisfactory nature of our own lives. That is certainly part of the learning curve of growing up, but I would also argue that social media has magnified our need to be able to do that ten-fold.

This remains an inherent part of my personal battle with social media. I think it is entirely correct for people to have boundaries in regard to what they share on social media, to decide to keep some of life's struggles to themselves, to protect their own privacy, and that of the people they love. However, that in turn does contribute to the falsehood of the perfect life, devoid of struggles or sadness. I suppose a perfectly curated Instagram feed has become the white picket fence of Gen Z. It preys on my mind a lot, as I do think my feed gives the impression of life being quite easy and straightforward. It's a combination of happy events, easy moments and often the facile – like the constant hair colour changes! In offering such a combination it belies many of the struggles that do go on behind the scenes.

I know my voice on social media has an element of elevated power as a result of having a large audience, and that audience is predominantly young women, who I think are consistently targeted as consumers to believe they want and need the latest thing. I have experienced this myself, and still do. I worry about that, and it is complicated trying to understand my role in perpetuating cycles of consumption. I wonder whether it is enough to be selective in the products I advertise, and genuinely to use them, because advertising is advertising. It is not always as obvious as the outlandish claims that are sometimes made, which indicate to me that a business is unscrupulously overreaching in its statements, in particular when it comes to self-care (from aura-cleansing candles to positive mental-attitude-inducing hairbrushes). There is nothing wrong with treating yourself to something that can make you feel good – I am very partial to a scented candle, particularly at Christmas – but to give the impression that such an item can solve all one's problems is disingenuous.

Equally, I don't want to belittle content that discusses make-up, beauty, fashion, clothing. I like it, and I watch plenty of it. I have always had an intention to do the odd make-up tutorial here and there, but whenever I come to film it I lose my nerve at the last minute. Many of the people who specialise in these areas also provide useful information, allowing consumers to be more responsible in their choices, whether in terms of eco-friendly brands or providing affordable 'dupes' for expensive products. Nor does it mean that the interests of those who produce such content are any less varied, multi-faceted or well-intentioned than anyone else's. Frequently, such platforms show a cross-section of information, from fashion, jewellery, and lifestyle to activism and causes they care about.

But even in trying to avoid promoting ridiculous products or services that I don't use, even in trying to be selective with the brands I work with, even in trying also to use my platform as a place where I can share information about the causes I care about, I constantly feel that I am walking a very a fine line, and I cannot ignore that there is a cumulative effect that comes from both knowingly and unwittingly using social media to sell material items. What I do know, is that when it comes to business, if the focus of that business is solely profit, the potential implications for individuals, be that their mental health or their bank balances, are often largely ignored. The fact that promotion can have a damaging effect on someone's self-esteem is at best an inconvenient side-effect of sales and marketing, and at worst a human facet that is exploited. Examining my complicity with, and existence within, that system is uncomfortable.

We live in a system that perpetuates the idea of winners and losers, and it is constantly reinforced that this is a necessary evil in order for progress to be made. I think the expression of this in the online world has been interesting. There is one particular word which, for me, comes up time and time again: shame. We are bombarded with the idea that we should feel ashamed for being losers, and that this state has nothing to do with things we cannot control, such as our genes or our opportunities. It is solely our responsibility to live up to the ideals that are presented to us. I should feel ashamed that I don't look like the people in the photographs. I should feel ashamed because I don't have this car, or that lifestyle. Those are the things that make people happy, and I just simply haven't got them.

Actually, all those things are only ever obtainable for a very small minority, and it is the idea that those things are more desirable, and therefore somehow necessary, is the damaging concept. The idea that you can only be happy when you have something only a tiny subsection of the population can actually achieve. We should not underestimate those prevailing voices, they can physically change the way we decide to look. They can alter our entire perspective of ourselves. We wear those effects like badges.

At the same time, it has inadvertently presented a solution to that problem, and that is presenting our own lives as better – more glamorous, more interesting, more exciting – than they are. Then we become the subject of another's envy rather than the envier. This is an inelegant solution that not only renders the online world a difficult place to navigate as you end up feeling your life is not good enough, it is as detrimental to you as it is to the viewer. That separation between your real life and your online life, leaves you feeling as if you have something to hide, or like your real life is shameful. The likes you receive on the life you are presenting only serve to underline how important it is to be that person, and that leaves you striving to be someone that is so two-dimensionally perfect, that they could only exist in the online world.

I don't think any of us necessarily feel we know exactly how to navigate the online world safely, to our own gain, rather than to our detriment, but I worry most about the young people who are exposed to this world. Social media remains in its infancy, and it feels there is very little institutionalised knowledge to transfer to the younger generation about how best to navigate the online world, and what to avoid.

And truthfully, in the prevailing winds of the online clickbait, what are we teaching the younger generation about which information may be important? You can have a news article about the siege in Idlib, with children covered in blood and rubble, right next to a post about the latest fast fashion trend accompanied by a funny meme. That juxtaposition is surely having an effect on our ability to process information. Equally, within articles there often seems a deliberate intent to juxtapose the important with the facile, such as the discussion of politicians making important decisions, accompanied by a full run down on what they were wearing. It feels like we are living in a post-factual time, and this has arisen from an interesting paradox.

Firstly, the people we would usually put our trust, namely political leaders, have often been exposed on such platforms, as they have provided a less-regulated avenue for investigative journalism to be disseminated. As these people have been exposed, our understanding of what the people at the top are willing to do to ensure they hold onto power, has left us deeply mistrusting of the information we are given through traditional channels. Suddenly, people who had been unable to run very real exposés had an opportunity to share the truth. However, these platforms also provide avenues for conjecture and speculation with very little to distinguish between these and genuine reportage, and which repeated enough times becomes 'fact'. They are also where clickbait articles that may or may not have their foundations in truth are found, and there is nothing to distinguish between the two. This exposure of truth, alongside the proliferation of the sensationalised and entirely incorrect, has made for a very confusing environment.

I think most people would agree that we have reached a point where social media poses a very real and immediate risk, in particular to young people. In May 2016, an eighteen-year-old woman live streamed her suicide on the platform Periscope.[13] She had announced in the days leading up to the video that she would be saying something sensational. In the video, she told the viewers that her ex-boyfriend had raped and beaten her, ostensibly because he hadn't taken responsibility for his actions, so she gave his contact details. Some of the comments appearing on the live feed were sympathetic, but many commented on the way she looked, on her piercings. Many called her ugly. Some called her a whore. And some told her to kill herself. She walked to a nearby train station. Even as she approached the station, whilst some of the commentators began to voice their concern, others continued to tell her to kill herself. She jumped in front of a train with

---

[13]   https://www.theguardian.com/news/2017/aug/29/the-first-social-media-suicide

the video still streaming, the screen went black but continued to record. The final seconds of the video show a paramedic picking up the phone, and pressing stop.

I find this story immeasurably sad for so many reasons. Perhaps there is a touch of her story that resonates with me. I feel like she was existing in a world at a time when being a young woman was desperately confusing. She apparently took issue with people on social media platforms, and found it fake and performative. Yet, at the same time she would post photos herself. I feel her confusion at the contradictory nature of the world, and perhaps even herself. I feel her drift from life's reality as it burdened her too much.

The part of the story I cannot understand, that I cannot even begin to fathom, are the people telling her to kill herself. It's illuminated in this story because of the utterly horrendous way it ends, but it is also something we see daily, and perhaps where it doesn't have such harsh and immediate consequences, it is not seemingly seen as problematic. But it is deeply problematic. The thing is, there are behaviours that are tolerated online, that simply would not be tolerated in the real world. If we walked down the street and a grown man was yelling expletives at a teenage girl, we would step in. There are so many instances where events simply wouldn't be socially acceptable.

Further to that, the online world provides avenues for real-world issues also to exist online, for example cyber bullying. There is, too, a worrying trend in digital self-harm, which is when people send themselves hate online, for example by creating ghost accounts from which they send themselves negative messages and comments. These have proved to be tricky topics to tackle in the public domain, since discussions about the toxic aspects of the online world invariably involve sharing details, and sometimes images and videos, which, although intended to show the risks, can then be popularised by the very people at risk.

Most of us are naive when it comes to social media, however knowledgeable we think we may be. Platforms were shaped by the whims and biases of the people behind them, and even they could not have anticipated the social disruption they would cause. I think one of the main issues is the lack of due diligence accorded to each new platform as it emerges. It just feels like discussions in the upper echelons of our leaders are woefully lacking. In particular, I think there is a huge disjoint at the moment in the knowledge of the people we expect to lead us politically, and their understanding of the various challenges and risks the rapidly evolving social media landscape presents. It is axiomatic that disruptive technology supersedes older processes and habits, and so for those who did not grow up with it, or perhaps still view it as frivolous, it is difficult for them to make informed decisions about policies and regulations. But so much socialising does now take place online, and the platforms on which this takes place are continually updating.

Our apps are not impartial in the way they appear to be, and that is perhaps why social media is so much more powerful than we give it credit for. It's funny, because a lot of the flaws of technology can hide in plain sight. Words like algorithms and metadata seem completely irrelevant to us, and that vernacular is important in creating a sense of separation from the interaction of artificial and human intelligence. The complexity of the human brain, of the counterintuitive thoughts we all have, is steadily being unpicked by technology. This is a risk in a world where so much of our weakness and doubts are what are used to sell us falsehoods of prerequisites for happiness.

When a seemingly impartial device is corroborating your fears and doubts, the effect is powerful. Marketing relies on us feeling inadequate. For example, selling anti-ageing products relies on us worrying about ageing, and so the fetishisation of youthfulness is a useful tool to push moisturisers and treatments claiming to stop or slow down what is a natural process. The online world can be used to identify what we are worried about, both on an individual and collective level, and then to target us with images or information that confirm our worries. This is designed to make us think we need things or services, to feel we are enough, otherwise the message is that we simply don't fit the mould which, in order to belong, we are meant to.

It's not just our ability to foresee the impact social media will have as a collective that is the tricky, it's also our ability as an individual. There have been countless times when I haven't realised information from my phone and laptop screen was having a huge influence on both my thought processes towards others, as well as towards myself. It is subtle, how our lives are shaped by the online world, I think because often we believe we see it as us sharing our real world online, rather than seeing the online world as affecting us in the real world. Social media often feels like we are reshaping the world around us, and to an extent we are, but the same is also happening in reverse i.e. social media is affecting what we will tolerate in the real world, and the choices we subsequently make. If your feed is full of click bait headlines that tell you it is alright to pry into other people's lives, that becomes normalised.

To return to the Milgram experiment, it is interesting how drastically the psychologists underestimated the number of people who would continue to administer electric shocks, apparently far beyond what they had been told were safe levels. It may be that their instructions, written down or presented to them, seemed too far from the actual events. Perhaps you read the start of this chapter, thinking there is no way I would do that. In almost all cases of the subjects continuing, they would still express their feelings of distaste for the experiment. They would sweat and clutch their hands, and say how they thought the experiment was wrong – but they kept going. What happens if someone is resetting the norms we have lived by in such a subtle way, that we don't even realise it is happening?

I think this is important because we are looking at the world around us for guidance, and at the moment the most pervasive voices remain at the core of apps and social media. Because it feels like they are guiding us, it is very easy for us to let them assume the burden of blame, they are the experimenter that is telling us what to do. Telling us we need to continue with the electric shocks. But there are people who are pounding on the wall, we can hear them with every story that discusses the negative effects of social media and mental health, and it is important that within that antagonistic online environment, we still keep sight of the impact we can have on people. That every click of the mouse on an abusive article, every nasty comment, every unsavoury DM has a very real effect on someone's life. Otherwise, how many of us will realise when we are administering a 450-volt shock to someone?

Chapter 10

Platforms for Good

―――――

There is an argument for social media as a platform for good. Many topics and issues that might otherwise have struggled to find an audience among certain demographic groups now have a means of doing so. The passage of information is opening up, and yet on the other side of that, for the most part there are still reservations over how effective clicktivism (the use of social media to support a cause) is in bringing about actual, measurable change.

There is also an argument that social media users often experience saturation point. Where before, we would have supported the charities that touched us personally, as well as perhaps occasionally sponsoring our friends or perhaps the child who lives across the hall from us, suddenly now people feel that they are constantly being asked to sponsor hundreds of people, some of whom we don't even know. In some ways, constant access to information can desensitise us to it. Equally, I think it's important that people feel that they can use that space to promote causes they believe in. I have particular charities and causes that are of interest to me, but I want to learn about others, and often it is people who themselves have a particular affinity with that cause who will publicise it online. That is what social media provides as a platform, and there is a difficult balance to be struck.

I do sometimes feel overwhelmed by the number of messages I receive daily to promote various fundraising pages and charities, as well the number that come through my agent. Sometimes that will just be to support certain specific campaigns, sometimes it will be discussions of longer-term involvement as an ambassador of that charity. The problem is you would love to help everyone, but it just simply isn't feasible. Furthermore, you can end up doing a lot of harm by not taking the time to review such requests with the attention they deserve.

I have tried to reach a balance with it. A big part of that for me is understanding my responsibilities to doing my own due diligence on which charities I support. Of course, with HALO that was relatively straightforward as I knew what was going on, on the ground, and where money would be directed. With others, I try and ensure I ask for the appropriate briefings, and do my own research. It is also important to me to serve the causes that I feel personally struck most by, but also where I think I can do the most good. A huge part of that has been from working in current, or post-conflict zones and having some kind of an understanding of the devastating effect conflict has on people's lives.

Platforms for Good

We continue to see a damaging and damning rhetoric around those who have been forced to flee their homes because of conflict. It should be blindingly obvious that people forced to leave their homes do not want to do so; indeed, many are so reluctant to go that they leave it until it is too late. They don't want to be so terrified that they will not survive at home, that they have to leave to some totally unknown place. It seems that there are some commentators online who struggle to imagine that displaced refugees might have had lives and homes that they loved. These critics seem to be entirely wrapped up in an egotistical idea that our lives are the best, and everyone wants them. That simply isn't true. What people who have been forced to flee war and oppression are asking for is their own lives back, and in the horrific meantime, a safe place to stay. This should be the bare minimum, and it's outrageous that it's not.

In that manner, I have seen how social media has been used as a force for good. One of the examples I've been lucky enough to be able to support is the Choose Love/ Help Refugees movement. I met Josie Naughton, co-founder and CEO of Choose Love/Help Refugees in the months immediately following *Love Island* in 2017. The first trip I took with her was to Calais. I met many people there, including unaccompanied children. To get out of a country that is currently in the midst of war, often you have to pay smugglers to get across the border and find passage onward. Many families cannot afford to send more than one member, and so often they will send their oldest son. In Calais, there were thirteen- and fourteen-year-old boys from Afghanistan that were entirely alone, living rough in the surrounding woods. By this time, the Calais Jungle, the main refugee camp in that area, had been destroyed, torn down by the authorities in October 2016. They were not allowed to create any permanent structures, they weren't even allowed tents. The French police were going into the woods almost every night/early morning, and would break the phones of those who had them (their only means of contacting family many miles away), and taking the sleeping bags and coats from people. These children were cold, hungry and frightened.

A couple of months later, in December 2017, a fifteen-year-old boy was run over by a truck in Calais, in an attempt to reach his brother in London. Abdullah was from Nangarhar province in Afghanistan. In the weeks after I read some of the backlash. Many were horrified, but some said things like 'it's his own fault, he shouldn't have been trying to come here illegally'. Abdullah should have been eligible to enter the UK legally under family reunification legislation. The issue at that time was that the procedures that have been put in place to protect vulnerable people, and those in need during times of conflict were not being administered in a timely or accessible fashion. The night Abdullah died on the motorway he didn't even want to be there. He only tried to board a UK-bound lorry because he and his cousin were so cold in the woods, that they felt they had no other choice. His cousin saw his body dragged by a lorry for 100 metres, before it drove away and left the crumpled, broken, crushed child in the road. A child that we let down. It's as simple as that.

Platforms for Good

Later, in 2018, I was able to join Josie and two of her colleagues from Choose Love/Help Refugees, Nico and Matty, on a trip to Turkey and Lebanon, to visit camps and projects along the Syrian border.

We sat with doctors who had been operating within cities under siege. We met women whose husbands had been missing for many years, possibly dead but perhaps imprisoned and tortured. We met so many people who were still living through the most desperate of times. I learnt so much from how Josie, Nico and Matty dealt with every person. How they spoke with love, passion and sorrow – but equally they shared jokes in the right moments, or listened as their friends suggested the best dishes to eat, or the right route to take through town to our next meeting. They saw them for the people they are. They did not patronise them with labels, nor force 'help' upon them that they didn't want – they asked what they needed, and then they really listened to the answers.

Everywhere we went I saw people respond to their kindness, where there could have been barriers, there were bridges, where there could have been misunderstanding there was communication. Not only that, but on this trip, I bonded with them as women. On long journeys we talked about everything from our relationships to how to set the world to rights. We shared bowls of pasta, drank wine and laughed at the silly things we said or did. They extended exactly the same compassion and interest to me as they did to every single other person. It is this that makes the Choose Love project so special, for truly it is a tale of what binds us all together as people, it is about humanity and, at its core, that is about love.

That's the one thing I have seen across every country where I have ever worked – how similar our key problems as people are: heartache, worry, grief, as well as qualities like hope and joy. Actually, it's these things that bind us together, that make us no different to another version of ourselves born in another place at another time. I know people, both near and far, who have had their world turned upside down. I have seen so much of the suffering that brings. Often, that is seemingly insurmountable pain, which never quite goes away but sits quietly and constantly in us, even when it is no longer visible on the surface. I believe that there is something important packed away in that ghost of suffering past, something that reminds us not moralise, not to simplify other's pain, not to reduce the problems of others, but to empathise, and understand.

It's not that I am seeking to justify pain and suffering, not for anyone. But I suppose I like the idea that we can give them meaning. That they don't need to be thrown aside or hidden away in the backs of our minds, to dwell on one cold, quiet and lonely night. The pain that we are all capable of feeling speaks to how powerful that suffering is, and the idea of being able to channel that power into feelings of commonality and connection is a comforting thought. Some people reading this now may be heartbroken. Many will be dealing with loss, or uncertainty about the future. For that I am truly sorry. But I think it's very special that even in those times of uncertainty and pain, you can provide certainty for someone else's future. The certainty that they will have a warm coat to wear through a bitter January spent in a cold tent, that they will have shoes to put on their son's feet so he doesn't walk in the snow barefoot, that they will have nappies to put on their baby daughter. A major part of my experience on that trip was the reminder that even when it feels as though the threads of our own lives are unravelling, we can bring certainty to someone else.

In the final few days, we travelled to the Beqaa valley, to visit Women Now. As we pulled up to the project headquarters, my phone received a message telling me we had arrived in Syria because we were so close to the border. On the drive in, I had seen several makeshift camps go by. Rudimentary shelters, usually wrapped in UNHCR tarpaulins for protection. Under Lebanese housing regulations, refugee shelters cannot be permanent structures. Those that are, usually are demolished by the Armed Forces. The camps we see are therefore informal, and inadequate to protect the men, women and children living there from brutally hot summers, and desperately cold winters. It is not always widely understood that the Lebanese winters are as cold as they are. In January 2018, fifteen people froze to death on their way across the Syrian/Lebanese border.[14]

But the day we arrive, the sun was brutally hot and the air hung heavy and moist. Women Now showed me their library, and then the rooms they used for language and vocational training, we also saw a small crèche where mothers could

---

[14] https://www.telegraph.co.uk/news/2018/01/22/fifteen-syrians-freeze-death-trying-flee-lebanon/

leave their children while in classes. The small building where they were based in the Beqaa Valley was full of warmth and laughter. We joined a sewing class, and one of the women came up and wrapped a scarf around my neck. In a room of toddlers, a young child held their arms up to me asking to be picked up. In one of the classrooms, a group of young women learnt how to do each other's hair in intricate updos, and though I couldn't understand the chatting, it was an environment as familiar as getting ready round one of my girlfriend's houses, and there was the same familiar buzz of conversation and laughter as three different conversations carried on at the same time.

War always leaves many widows. The Syrian conflict was further characterised by arbitrary detention, and thus many women became the sole providers for their families.

Some of these women had never been given the opportunity to learn many skills because they were seen as typically male, such as driving. Many had never had access to education at all. Now these women had been left to look after their households alone, they were extremely vulnerable in many ways. Women Now worked to help them build the vocational skills they needed in order to financially provide for their families, as well as socially empowering them in a way many had not experienced before.

The other day, I found something that I had written in the days after I got back from the trip:

It has taken me a little time to write this. Partly because I have felt busy (which is a whole different thing to being busy). But also, because I have experienced the same feeling I often have when I return from a trip – an everyday melancholy that makes the whole world feel grey, in amongst the joy of seeing friends and family again. The world is hazy again. Because the thing is, you can sit and listen to someone tell you the stories of their loved ones being tortured, you can watch videos of babies being bombed in their incubator coffins, you can hear stories of bravery and in that moment, you can react appropriately. You can tell them how sorry you are, that you will do everything in your power to help them out. But slowly, you realise that what you can give, is simply not enough. I cannot express the sheer anger you feel as you watch a campaign of misinformation gather traction. It is unbelievably irresponsible to spread such information with no thought to the innocent who have already died, and those who WILL die. No ifs, no buts, for many there is no hope left.

Since then, I have watched from a distance as misinformation has been disseminated on Twitter and Instagram, and other online platforms. I have watched as Russian proganada has tried to suggest that the Syrian civil war is a two-sided conflict, meanwhile the Russian-backed Assad regime attacks have intensified, and the targeting of civilians has continually escalated.

Against such a powerful force, for those inside Syria, they perhaps considered their greatest ally was their ability to capture the reality of the situation. With devices in the hands of ordinary people, footage capturing the reality of what was going on, has been seen right from the beginning of the protests in Aleppo. You have to wonder if those trapped inside thought their phones were their lifelines. This was the way they would tell the world what was actually happening. I've seen films like *For Sama* and *The Cave* conscientiously document the real, human experience of war. This was how they could capture videos of children who were victims of chemical attacks gasping to death in their parent's arms. This is where they could show the full horror of those trapped amongst the rubble. This is where they could show the relentless airstrikes targeting hospitals and other health facilities. They captured it, and did everything in their power to get that information out there. It has been perhaps the most documented war of all time, and still the world's eyes turned away.

I suppose I wondered how much of the information that is now able to be collected and disseminated on social media is actually taken seriously at a political level. How much of that information is seen as legitimate, and does it really inform decision-making. There still does not seem to be a genuine movement to reconsider what our responsibilities are both to those still under siege in Syria, and to the millions that have been displaced, even though their fate has been corroborated by respected foreign correspondents. Perhaps from a political standpoint, it is considered enough for us to be on the right side of history on social media. To say the right things on Twitter. It's not enough though, it's woefully inadequate for the parents desperately trying to keep their children alive.

In fact, in January 2020, we found out as part of the Brexit deal that we would no longer be honouring refugee child reunification with their families. The House of Lords tried to make an amendment to the Brexit bill, led by Baron Alf Dubs, who came to Britain himself as a child refugee in 1939 as part of the Kindertransport. The other Jews he had known in Prague who were unable to escape were taken to concentration camps; very few survived. Despite the House of Lords amendment, it was overturned by parliament and the Brexit bill passed without provision for reuniting child refugees with their families. It seems no number of horrific images, of children washed up on foreign shores, or frozen to death in ill-equipped camps, or lying with crushed skulls under piles of rubble and dust, is enough.

That's the problem with social media as a platform for good. We can see children painfully gasping their last breaths, and not realise that that is a reality that is happening elsewhere. It could never have been imagined a few decades ago, how much access we have to the reality of the suffering of others, and yet it can feel like it is making very little difference, and we are losing our ability to take in information without moralising or reducing the problems of others. In part, this is resulting from compassion fatigue, where continued exposure to traumatic images can contribute to emotional exhaustion and ultimately a diminished capacity to feel concern for others.

Somehow, it seems things like that can play out before our eyes, but there is a sense of removal from it. Perhaps it is because so much online is sensationalised, that it is hard to see anything with the gravitas it deserves, not only due to compassion fatigue steadily numbing people to the horrors seen online, but also because of the way our home pages and news feeds present information online, and the constant juxtaposition between the facile and the dreadfully serious – as mentioned earlier in Chapter 9. There are regularly articles about life-threatening situations, right next to popular culture gossip and features.

So, when people ask me if I believe social media is a platform for good, the truth is I can't really give a straight answer. I would much rather use it as a platform for talking about what I think is genuinely important for other people to know (that of course means different things to different people). I love it when you can really tell someone's passion from a page, be that in beauty, baking, animals, writing or anything really. I think Choose Love/Help Refugees (and many other charities, as well as reporters) does a huge amount of good through its online media outlets and has held at its core the importance of communicating information that is necessary, but perhaps this era of sensationalism has eroded our ability to identify what is truly devastating.

Perhaps we are also limited in our ability to imagine a world in which we don't reside. In a world that simply doesn't square away, unlike the neatly laid-out feeds of Instagram.

Chapter 11

Anxiety

———

I worry about things a lot. I can check my hair curlers are off six times before I leave the house, and still decide I need to go back to make sure they are definitely off. I'll lie awake, convincing myself that I've left the little electric heater on in the room I use as an office, even though I have carefully and deliberately turned it off and told myself in that moment to remember that I have done so. I'll run up and down the stairs checking the oven is off, convincing myself that the last time I switched it off, I actually switched it on by accident.

Back during my time with HALO in Zimbabwe, on occasions when I was working in the office in Harare I would drive a very old Land Rover between the office and the HALO house. The driver's door did not close properly, and so every time I made a left-hand turn, I would have to grab the inside door handle just as I began to turn to stop it swinging open and out, and then slamming shut as I began to drive straight again. The steering was also incredibly stiff, so I would have one hand turning the wheel to the maximum to the left, and the other hand grasping the door handle. It was comical anyway, but I added to the ridiculousness of it all by creating the most absurd scenarios in my head, like my rucksack somehow finding its way off the back seat, into my lap as I drove and then spilling out into the road. Even at night, in the exceptionally secure HALO house within its gated compound, I would wake up and imagine I could hear the vehicle being driven off.

I'm not particularly creative, but I do have an incredibly overactive worst-case-scenario imagination, but for all the times that I can now reflect on and see that I was being ridiculous, in the moment, my worst-case scenario perception seems entirely real. Often, this makes it hard to communicate with those around me, because this idea that the most unrealistic, extreme outcome is the one that I expect to happen is so unfathomable to them. Indeed, when I think about being anxious, the first thing I think about is feeling lonely. Anxiety for me is a perpetual fear of being rejected, and in turn, is an unending longing for acceptance and connection. But anxiety is cruel, in that the very thing it makes you feel you need, it stops you being able to attain. Thus, it is able to perpetuate its cycle, and trap your mind in an unending state of discomfort, and your body in high alert. It gets what it wants by telling you what you need and not allowing you to have it.

Often when I feel lonely, my social interactions, both in

real life and in the online world, are tinged with the sense of being mocked. It starts as nagging doubt at the back of my brain, 'oh that thing I said was really stupid', 'oh that joke I made wasn't as funny as I thought it was', and hurtles towards summations such as 'everyone at that party thought I was really boring', 'everyone at that dinner thought I shouldn't have made that inappropriate joke', 'everyone at that meeting noticed when I was interrupted, and didn't stand up for myself, although they were probably hoping I would be interrupted because I wasn't saying anything helpful anyway'. At worst, this idea that people are mocking me becomes the idea that people are treating me with disdain. Finally, ultimately, I add all of this up in my head until I feel like I have been rejected.

The thing that no one really tells you, or never told me anyway, is how anxiety will interact with every other part of your world. With your work. With your relationship with alcohol. With sex and relationships. My anxiety was heavily related to fear of human interaction, even the idea of attending pre-drinks was fraught with 'what if' questions, despite being in what should have felt like a safe and familiar environment among close friends. In the lead up, I would have this feeling of foreboding. I feel anxious before attending social occasions. I think this is more understandable in the context of the public events to which Jamie and I have been invited since *Love Island*. I'm sure the glamour and excitement of premieres and parties appeals to some, but equally I know that many people recognise the nerve-racking aspects of a red-carpet occasion. I suppose what people often find less easy to understand is why my anxiety should be equally as bad whether attending a friend's party or a premiere. If anything, I would say that I actually get more anxious before events at which there will be people I know well, or if there will be friends of friends there. Before I am even there, I imagine myself saying the wrong thing, or making a joke and no one laughing.

The easiest and most obvious fix for this at that time was having a drink before I had to be in any social situation. Rarely, was this just one drink. Then while I was at whatever social occasion it might be, my brain would still be firing on all cylinders. Frantically trying to work out if I had said or done the right thing. If the people around me liked me. If I'd committed some kind of terrible social gaffe. The only way to quiet these voices was to drink more – more and more. But of course, this could never lead to anything good. All too often, I found myself waking in the morning with no recollection of how the night ended. Had I offended someone? Made a complete and utter fool of myself?

No one tells you that when you are terrified of every social situation, how tempting it will be to have a couple of drinks before you go, and then with every awkward situation, with every moment of self-criticism while you are there, how having another drink seems like the easy fix until you are far too inebriated to make good decisions, but, as you are an anxious person, those bad decisions will haunt you, in the midst of a cold night as you lie awake and wonder once again why you are such a terrible person. Throughout life, I have constantly felt as though I am slightly more melancholy or more downbeat than my peers. Like I'm always on the verge of sinking into a sustained period of misery and to avoid that I would cling to any lifeboat I could find, whether that be the comforting numbness that too many Jägerbombs brought, or the attention of another person. I have dealt with different addictions in my life, but the most notable of these has been how I become addicted to people, and the affection and approval they can provide. This need for validation from others has, at times, utterly ruled my life.

Funnily enough, I am often told I don't have an addictive personality, this is because I can pick up smoking and stop again as easily as I started. I have gone for long periods of my life without drinking. But that is not because I have 'conquered' any of these addictions. It is because they were never really physical addictions, it was not my body that needed the cigarette but my mind. They were psychological crutches propping up a broken and fragile sense of self. I often experience an anxious paranoia, that manifests as a feeling of intense unease. Sometimes, this sense of impending doom casts such a shadow over the world that any escape from this is persuasive, a beacon of hope at the end of the tunnel, which so often has turned out to be a mirage.

For a long time, I thought it was entirely normal to spend a proportion of every day contemplating humiliation and rejection. In fact, I'd go so far as to say that this is the default state for me, and has been for as long as I can really remember. Although I thought this was the status quo for me, I failed to appreciate that other people also felt like that. For one thing, I knew people close to me often found my anxiety annoying, because of how it affected my behaviour. I could tell it made me frustrating to be around, as I would often expect the worst to happen. I would decide people didn't like me, that comments were meant to be cruel rather than kind, that people were being intentionally hurtful towards me. It felt like I was battling against the world, and yet to most other people that appeared as some kind of martyrdom, that I was determined to put myself through, and was entirely unnecessary.

I began to try and hide the signals of anxiety, and instead internalised my feelings of foreboding, rendering me shy and quiet, and in turn people perceived that as snobbish and aloof. At the crux of the issue for me was self-esteem, and what I built mine upon, but admitting that in itself felt like I was failing. The last thing I wanted to do was to discover that the anxiety I dealt with on a day to day basis was entirely self-inflicted. I already hated myself for allowing negative thoughts to take over my brain. Painful experiences in life are to be expected, but the misery I felt was often far more to do with continuing to perpetuate thought cycles, which constantly reminded me of painful experiences I had been through. I not only allowed these to accumulate over time, I also let them feed the idea that the world was out to get me. As much as I was struggling with painful experiences of the past, often it was anticipation of further suffering that was my greatest problem and fear. I think in some bizarre way, I was looking back and trying to relive those feelings of pain, so that next time (and I always felt that the next time was just around the corner) I would be prepared for it.

I do think this, in part, related back to the problem-solving brain. In a way, you are trying to go back to resolve things that have already happened and which caused you pain. Part of you thinks, if I go over this enough, I'll find some way to change what happened; I simply couldn't let the past rest. I covered it over and over again, walking down familiar pathways day and night, knowing that the only outcome would be a leaden feeling of failure in my chest.

As much as you can't resolve things, this is also not the way to prepare for future pain. I punished myself daily, to the point where small incidents that I should have been able to cope with became unbearable. It doesn't make life any easier for you, but more so than that, it is one of the behaviours that those around me find immensely difficult to deal with. Everything was a drama, everything went on and on. Even when I tried to mask how I was feeling, it would inevitably come out in an argument or in a moment that really shouldn't have been a big deal.

I suppose from my personal experience, I can only really speak of anxiety (and the possible PTSD I mentioned in Chapter 5), although I do wonder about the periodic moments of dark feelings in my life. Perhaps that was depression, but I've always struggled to confront the fact that I might need help and it is next to impossible to self-diagnose something, which warps your self-awareness so cruelly.

What I do know is this. The symptoms of difficulties with mental health are often really, truly unpleasant and complicated, and such difficulties can manifest themselves in entirely different ways for different people. They can result in aggressive, competitive, self-centred behaviour, as much as being characterised by a quiet retreat from the world. However, the former are not as widely discussed in the media as being part of mental health difficulties, instead there seems to be more of a focus on palatable and understandable behaviour, such as shyness, which is easier to recognise as fearfulness. I do think that is what this rise in mental health awareness has sorely lacked, and I worry that our understanding of behaviour that might indicate a need for help is being limited to what is considered socially acceptable. In short, I think we need to be wary of a damaging message that can be sent by this very two-dimensional understanding of mental health that you can be depressed, you can be anxious, you can have PTSD, but only if it fits with our understanding of it. Only if it fits with what we allow – and the torment of mental illness is the exact opposite of that.

Tim Minchin, the Australian comedian, singer, songwriter and actor, gave a brilliant commencement address at the University of Western Australia in October 2013, which can be found on YouTube. In it, he talks about taking your opinions outside and bashing them with a cricket bat. You've got to be open to change, to a changing perspective of the world around you but equally to an evolving version of yourself. To the totally terrifying thought that you may not become the person you thought you would become. This ability to be open to change is only made more difficult in a world where everything is capture and magnified online. Anyone who has any kind of internet presence, is being watched in some way. There is something intensely exposing about that, which allows next to no space for failure. People watch you grow physically, mentally and emotionally. Not only that, but through social media they are provided the space to draw judgements on this, and that is intensely scary. I think this constant level of both scrutiny and judgement very closely relates to high levels of anxiety in young people. The influence of both internal and external voices was something that I neglected to notice in my understanding of my own anxiety, and possible depression. In part, my anxiety was due to the way my brain worked, how I file away the mistakes I have made, and also the way I blame myself for just not feeling as happy as everyone else around me. But it is also partly to do with the external voices.

My greatest fear about the way mental health is addressed on social media is that we are actually beginning to erode the knowledge we have about mental health in a public forum because we are not relating the actual difficult symptoms and often ugly behaviours associated with mental health struggles, because they cannot be placed tidily in a neat little box. For people who suffer with mental health issues, reducing our understanding of mental health in a wider sense also reduces and simplifies our understanding of individuals. In fact, it is indicative of a wider trend to ignore the complexities and flaws of human nature in general. If we acknowledge only the good or acceptable, and never the bad or difficult, then people begin to hide away in the shadows at the time when they need love, forgiveness and acceptance the most. The times when I have been the worst version of myself have been when I was desperately wrestling with anxiety. I had an almost deranged thought process, which made perfect sense to me, but meant I acted in a way that was irrational, since I was processing the information I took in from the world around me through an anxious and paranoid lens.

Of course, on social media, whenever a particular topic gains attention, there will be those who seek to counter it, and so alongside this discussion of being more open about mental health struggles, we have seen the opposing viewpoint also discussed in the public domain, which often involves the gaslighting of those with mental illness. In particular, there has been repeated use of the term 'snowflake generation' in a derogatory fashion, often invalidating the experiences of those with mental illness, and insinuating that people who experience mental illness allow themselves to succumb to it because of an absence of willpower. For example, discussions about how we are 'mollycoddling' a generation to think it is 'okay to have feelings'. But I think all evidence shows that young people are growing at a time where there are significant challenges to their mental health, that will then result in a greater number of people struggling – and that is not their fault. It's not a lack of willpower. Firstly, if you are growing up in this moment in time, you are being scrutinised more than ever before, and that brings with it a plethora of confusing and terrifying emotions. Secondly, the amount of distressing information available online about the wider world is huge, including very real issues that affect their future. Frequently, we see the younger generation actively engaged in causes but they have not been given any of the tools to deal with the emotional stress that this places on them, nor about the uncertainty they may be realising their future holds. Thus, the way anxiety is dealt with across the media means that often the most troubled will continue to retreat to the shadows, will still battle alone, all the while being told that 'it's okay to talk about it', while everything else is signifying to them that they shouldn't.

One thing I will say, is that whatever you are dealing with, there are a myriad of mental health difficulties that can interchange and interlock in different ways at different times. Whatever you are dealing with, it is hard. It is hard work getting up every day, and finding a way to work through it. Some days you will feel like you are taking a step forward, some weeks will feel like a huge step back. There will be mornings you wake up feeling so much better, like the breath is suddenly allowed to fill your lungs again, only for the wind to be knocked out of you mid-morning by the tiniest of things like an email from your boss, or a friend not replying to your text and suddenly it can feel like you are back at square one.

I have talked about anxiety as being part of the reason I strived to desensitise myself, almost removing myself from own self. That's because at the very height of your anxiety, everything feels like it is sharply pointed straight at you. An article that has nothing to do with you, can feel like it was entirely written to make you feel bad. So too, can an Instagram post that has nothing to do with you.

If I'm honest, sometimes I also feel like this when I see discussions of anxiety on social media or in the press. It makes me panic, as I feel like mine doesn't fit neatly into the box it should. It feels so messy. It feels like I can talk about certain aspects of it, but not of others, and that the darker sides of it should be tucked away, out of sight. That the obsessive checking must be turned into a joke. That the irrational thought processes must only affect me and never the people around me, and so must be kept solely inside my own head, where they just go around and around. I feel I am allowed to talk about anxiety, so long as I am expressing it in a particular way, to make it seem like a somewhat light and easy burden to carry, perhaps even a comical one.

Yet I still feel that anxiety in its weightiest of times, when it hangs around me like a heavy cloak, must be a quirky little fashionable coat that hides my flayed skin beneath it. It is something I feel I should wear lightly in order to fit in.

Chapter 12

A Strong Woman?

Early in 2019, I was hit by the pre-thirty panic. I nosedived straight back into a crisis of confidence. I wanted to ball up in my room watching whatever Netflix show I find most comforting. I wanted to turn the heating up really high, because I know it's the only way I will feel warm. I wanted to wear my comfiest clothes, everything with holes in that has been washed too many times, somewhere in that soft fabric I think I'm going to find the comfort I'm seeking.

This happens to me in cycles; as my life reaches a steadier, more predictable, and usually more comfortable equilibrium, the comfort and stability become almost instantly uncomfortable. Usually this is the point when I will run, because that is the point when I begin to feel that I have slipped into someone else's life. The time when I come home and open the front door and recognise nothing as my own. Or when I slip into bed each night and the sheets feel like someone else's, and I am overcome with worry that I have somehow ended up in the wrong place. And the worst is when I'm told I'm in the right place – that I am clever, or good at what I'm doing. That is when I set out on not necessarily a self-destructive route, but certainly a counterproductive one.

I just couldn't balance myself. It was similar to the feeling of social dislocation I had in the months leading up to my decision to go on *Love Island*, having come back from Kabul and, before that, Zimbabwe. The only way I can explain it, is it's like when you make a joke and it doesn't land, or your group of friends is talking about someone being generous/nasty/funny and you're not sure you agree but everyone else does – and you get this really deep sense of unease. You think the world has shifted and you don't fit into your space anymore. I think we spend a lot time during our lives trying to fit neatly into spaces others have assigned us – I certainly have.

I had this unsettling feeling of being out of place. I find it quite hard to talk about, because life becomes pretty terrifying when it becomes unbearable to be with yourself. Over time those negative thoughts accumulate until you're so far away from yourself that the only way to keep going is to fit into the space it feels like the world is telling you is right, which in turn leaves you feeling more dislocated than ever.

As I unpicked these feelings in the lead up to my thirtieth birthday, I began to look back over my life to try to map the intersection of where the internal voices that told me I couldn't do things, met the external voices that told me I couldn't do things, ultimately to discover how I had still ended up on the path that I had. Often the hard time I have felt I have been given has actually been from the internal voice in my own head, that I perceived as being entirely my own. However, the reason that voice is as persuasive as it is, is because it is an amalgamation of every voice you have ever respected, or been influenced by, or are afraid of, and the things they would say to you spoken back within your own head by your own voice.

It can feel as if we are always getting things wrong, and it's absolutely exhausting. We live in a society where everything you see tells you that you should care about the way you look, you're constantly overwhelmed by images in social media and magazines of what is considered desirable. Yet, if you do care, you are also wrong for caring about the way you look. If you take too long getting ready, you are vain and misguided. So much of the blame is laid at the feet of the individual, and I see this consistently across various issues, both big and small. With regards to plastic consumption, it is up to the individual to change their habits, despite the fact that surely the most effective way to mitigate over-consumption is through legislation that puts the responsibility upon large companies to look for alternatives. Yet if you are, say, a busy mum who forgets her water bottle one day and has to grab a plastic one from the corner shop, it is you who feels guilt and shame; you are the one who is getting it wrong.

When I was growing up, my parents' room had a huge bookcase in that lined one wall (it probably wasn't actually that big, but I was tiny). In fact, when I first went to school, an older girl wrote a letter home that said a new girl had joined that was no bigger than a fire extinguisher – we used to use one of those larger size fire extinguishers to block open the huge, heavy front door of the school – this is almost definitely NOT allowed these days, but in that time, I happily toddled past it daily. I used to read very quickly and would regularly run out of new books to read before our next visit to the library so I would go and look at this shelf, and try and figure out if there were any that looked interesting. I was probably about six or seven at the time, so lots of them looked boring and old to me, but occasionally I would come across one I might like, and I loved the idea that I was reading grown up books.

One of the books on the shelf that always caught my eye was titled *Men are from Mars, Women are From Venus*. The title was split into two types of font. The first part was in strong, angular, dark blue capitals; the second half was in dark pink upper- and lower-case italics. I kept seeing these divisions everywhere. In the films I saw, the books I read, the colour my name was typed in on the label above my school coat hook. In the way I wore skirts to school, even though I hated tights. In the list of professions once written down for me, when I said I didn't know what I wanted to be when I was older. In the end, I didn't pick anything from the list. Instead, I went for a farmer like my grandad, or an astronaut because I'd just done a project on Neil Armstrong. Time and time again, I felt a sense of discomfort and confusion at my place within the world, I felt I was being strong-armed towards a path that had already been decided for me.

When I was young I loved party dresses with puffy

sleeves, and floral patterns, at the time I was also obsessed with Dennis the Menace. I loved ballet but would frequently complain about going to class because I was shy, so my mum would tuck a *Beano* in my little case with my ballet shoes as a treat. Later, I spent a year with a bowl cut hairstyle wearing boys clothes. I also went through a stage of crop tops and sparkly jeans. I read a lot, and could be quiet and studious. I spent huge amounts of time shut in my bedroom on my own reading. Equally, I really liked being outdoors. There was a burn (small river in Scots) between our garden and the field behind it, and I liked to paddle along it and pretend I was going on an adventure. I loved going on shopping trips with my aunt. I loved driving the combine harvester with my grandad, and helping him out on the farm. I loved baking biscuit cake and Millionaire's shortbread with my grandma. So many of these activities are considered gendered – but as a child I just did what I enjoyed, and it was never really questioned. Rather, these varying interests were seen as the folly of childhood.

Slowly, as I grew older, the space where I could write my life grew smaller and narrower. The margins grew wider, and in them were judgement and red marks against my choices, adjusting me until I fit into a two-dimensional character that could be neatly categorised. It was no longer acceptable to be a mysterious mix of characteristics, now I had to 'grow up' and figure out the type of women I wanted to be, and the different versions of these women seemed so limited.

Our unconscious bias is built by the world we see around us, giving rise to prejudice, and impacting the way we view people. That also pertains to our perception of ourselves, and the ability to underestimate our own capabilities is often deeply rooted in what we have been exposed throughout our life. This may mean you feel out of place somewhere where your skills and beliefs are entirely appropriate for the job in hand, simply because of the information you have been fed about the 'right type' of person. For me this caused immense personal confusion, as my mind was still striving to fulfil what was truly important to it, unaware that it was bound by external societal structures that affected my perception of what 'type' I was.

In the last couple of decades, it has felt as if the narrative has changed somewhat and we have seen the emergence of a bigger range of female characters; the strong woman, the hot mess, the straight-laced Jane. But trapped within a real life patriarchal system, or written and created by men or indeed woman whose whole life has been influenced by the male gaze, all too frequently these turned into reductive characters that were palatable. The hot mess whose success has a quirky, almost accidental quality to it, gives the idea that she has 'not got above her station'. The strong woman wears so easily the marks of masculinity to which we are already accustomed, that they are able to merge inoffensively into the cultural landscape. And Jane? She, of course, turns out to be more sexy than strait-laced.

In fact, that 'strong woman' was exactly the archetype that I tried so hard to emulate. From when I was very young, I have heard people mock being 'feminine'. I remember so clearly a male friend making fun of a woman who had turned up to camping trip they were going on with a suitcase, wearing high heels. Yes, it was unsuitable attire really, but it is what she liked wearing, and truly so many of the aesthetic trappings that we feel bound to were created by the male gaze. Despite these being largely male created ideals of femininity, they are the same scores that are used to undermine and degrade, and it cuts both ways. If you aren't feminine enough, that too is a source of ridicule. Not only has the ideal of feminine been cut from an incredible narrow design, but you have to be exactly the right amount of feminine, in the right place, at the right time.

For a long time, I felt like I could almost achieve that balance. There was period of my life when I was able to drink a relatively high amount of alcohol, and be outwardly unaffected. I was able to eat a large amount of food, and maintain a slim physique. I could keep up, whilst still fulfilling a widely accepted standard of the petite, white young woman. And I was not blind to this fact. In fact, often I tried to develop my skills in being able to slip, not only unobtrusively into a man's world, but pleasingly. I did it a lot and I'm ashamed of it. I laughed at sexist jokes because it was the way to fit in, and I disregarded the guilt I felt as ME being overly reactive, because everyone else around me thought it was alright, and not doing any harm in the long run. I allowed people to think it was all right to compliment me in inappropriate situations; sometimes I was flattered by it, and thought it a sign of my ability to slot neatly in without being disruptive. I thought this was me getting it right, that I had found the right way to fit into this world.

However, in hindsight I realise what I was actually learning was how to exist in a world within the parameters that others saw fit, rather than laying claim to my own legitimate space. I wasn't really existing as my actual self, or thinking about what would make me happy. I was thinking about how to make those around me happy and how to be accepted by them. In fulfilling the ideals that had been presented to me rather than the values that served me best, I always felt as if I was being pitted against other women. It felt as if there was always a chance someone would come along who could fit in better than I was, and that if they appeared then I was entirely replaceable.

In the last decade, these stories have changed somewhat, but for a while it was still rare to see truly nuanced, and thus real, female characters. Some people were ahead of the game on this. The BBC comedy *Fleabag* broke not only the fourth wall – the invisible screen that usually separates the audience from the actor – but also shattered the illusion of women as two-dimensional characters. Phoebe Waller-Bridge created someone in whom we could all see something of ourselves. The titular character was deceptively humorous (on the surface at least), but showed enormous depth and nuance (particularly unusual in the realm of sitcom); exhibiting truisms of the female experience, as did her sister. The relationship between these two women was extraordinarily compelling, and not the stuff of an oversimplified sisterhood that we have seen so often in print and online media. As we watched them navigate the fine lines of family, friendship and womanhood, it felt wonderfully real, and honest.

A Strong Woman?

The information we consume has become bite-sized, and Twitter and Instagram feeds are full of clickbait headlines and blink-and-you'll-miss-it images of what we should look like and who we should be. These, by their very nature, cannot give the full story, and in a similar way to twenty-four hours of life on *Love Island* being neatly edited down into a one-hour TV show, the reality of the situation is distilled down until it is hopelessly simplified. This creates assumptions and myths about the best possible way to be a woman, which simply do not echo an imperfect reality. They back women into a corner through shaming. We see it with regard to so many parts of life, one of the most poignant examples being the experience of motherhood, where judgements and generalisations are so often made about what is both a diverse and an intensely personal experience.

We have been served unrealistic ideals of what being a woman is about by almost every avenue of information – books, TV, magazines, and possibly even by family and friends. Ideals that do nothing to serve our feelings of fulfilment, or our happiness, or our sense of freedom as any unified ideal of being a woman disregards the fact that we are all unique. Of course, it is important to note that in no way do I want to isolate or degrade those who have chosen societies idea of traditional activities based on their own desires – that pursuit of what brings you fulfilment is, as always, to be applauded. The issue is that we often hear everyday activities, when conducted by women, distilled down and described as 'sexy' or 'cool', as if what they are doing is only for outward appreciation, rather than focussing on the fulfilment it brings to them. No life should be reduced to a performative version of itself, male or female. People are contradictory. This includes women.

I think that's why I spent much of my life in a state of confusion over what being a 'strong' version of myself meant. So much of our understanding of strength is tied to values that uphold a masculine ideal and eviscerate the strength that sits at the core of a woman's sensibility. All the time I spent focussed on becoming a socially accepted 'strong person', and subsequently a 'strong woman' distracted me from focussing on the aspects of myself that were strong, not weak. In being so celebrative of antiquated displays of strength, in a stiff upper lip and actually physical prowess, we have actually made it seem that other skills, such as compassion, that are not necessarily opposing but different, are weak. 'Man up' I heard time and time again, from the world around me, echoing in every corner of the Twittersphere. I am absolutely not saying that all the things we currently see as strong, are weak, nor the other way around. I am more advocating for a broader interpretation, that accommodates traits regardless of whether they are seen as typically male or female.

Eventually, so afraid was I to show my vulnerability my strengths actually became points of weakness because I refused to embrace them. I was so scared to show emotion, or to communicate feelings, and instead desperately sought to find a way to be more of what I thought the world expected of me. Needless to say, this did not work. Not only that but it did not empower me, it only served to show me where I fell short and made me feel even more out of place. It also played completely against my actual strengths, of thoughtfulness and empathy, and I was left feeling inadequate and wholly undeserving of the life I led.

It is only now I wonder if 'man up', when said to either a man or women, is ever truly really helpful? In its very essence it undermines the notion of women being strong. Not only that, but this idea that manning up is not expressing your emotions is surely damaging to men who need to be able to communicate their need for help. Not only are they not being taught the skills to do so, they are being actively sent a message that it is not acceptable to demonstrate that need. This seems incredibly damaging, especially given suicide continues to be the biggest killer of men under forty-five in the UK. It is important not to simplify the reasons why a person may commit suicide, but equally it's important to recognise that closing the avenues anyone feels to expressing their inner struggles has consequences, and we will never be able to move forward constructively if we do not seek to face difficult issues head on, rather than neatly brush them under the carpet with a simple 'man up'.

Slowly, we have sanded away the rough edges and corners of life to make an easier, smoother world, not realising in doing so we are making a world that we could never hope to belong in because we are all so ragged-edged. Our society has written and re-written generations of history so that that one particular ideal sits fully at the fore; a strong and attractive person, and all too often that person has been male. Women simply cannot thrive in a world that venerates only the feminine, but so too can no one truly thrive in a world that denigrates the flawed and imperfect (given that that is what we all are). Those who do not neatly fit into our expectations, because we have created the idea of a perfect world that in reality does not exist.

You are neither a hot mess nor a straight-laced Jane, nor even a strong woman. You are person, every bit as diverse as you should be. You are a myriad of mistakes, a catalogue of success. You are going to have times when it feels like the storm has passed, and the winds will suddenly begin again from a totally different direction. And you will emerge as gloriously windswept as in the past, with a fresh layer of dust covering you that needs to be sorted through and stored in your foundations until you are undeniably, irrepressibly you. There will be no end to this cycle, nor should there be, as Tim Minchin so eloquently stated, we should be looking to continually evolve as we learn more about ourselves and the world around us. It is worth remembering that that is true for ourselves, but also the people around us too.

I didn't honestly feel strong enough to write this book. It opened up wounds that I thought I had closed, and I became increasingly overwhelmed. The familiar aches and pains in my heart started to appear again. It felt like when you are training for a marathon, where every little niggle in your body is exposed.

Reading for me is like breathing, the words are the air that fill my heart and lungs, and sustain me as my body struggles through yet another day. They are my escape. They are a place where I can always find solace, be that in the weekly column of a favourite writer, or in the oldest most thumbed book on my shelf.

But writing, especially writing about myself, is like running. It is a painful, uncomfortable experience, viscerally so. It has forced me to confront very unpleasant truths about the persona I am versus the person I want to be, and the only thing I can hope is that I share that feeling with others. I strived for such a perfect life, and was completely blindsided when things went wrong, particularly when, for the most part, they were because of me. It has perhaps forced me closer to a degree of acceptance that life is not the linear struggle I anticipated it to be; we do not pass one aspect of it and then move on to the next. The reality will be far more complex than that.

I knew from a young age, I wanted to try and do things right, and I was so scared of the world where it felt so easy to get things wrong. As I grew older, from my teens onwards, I felt there was a weight associated with being a woman in environments that did not always feel like they welcomed them, I felt there was more pressure on me to do things perfectly, and of course I didn't, which always felt like a heavy weight upon my shoulders. I suppose I felt that every foot I put wrong as a woman meant something more than a personal mistake. It felt so much bigger than me. Yet it also felt that the blame was squarely placed on my shoulders as an individual – that there was something wrong with me, and never with the systems I was existing in. I let all that harden me in a way that made me believe in a lesser version of myself, as though the world seemed to inspire an endless feeling of not being good enough, and that made me underestimate myself. Perhaps that is the real insight I have gained from this. Don't underestimate people, no matter how much the world makes you feel that you should, and don't underestimate yourself.

One of the things I always found it hardest to do was to make a fool of myself, in front of anyone. If I did, it haunted me. If I asked a stupid question, I wouldn't sleep that night for thinking about it. Making a fool of yourself in front of people is one of the most important ways to form truly intimate relationships, with friends and family, as well as romantic partners. It's how you test the bounds of a friendship, how you realise that people will be there no matter what. So not being able to do so obstructed my ability to feel comfortable in friendships – indeed, in relationships of all kinds. And it stopped me doing a lot of things I would have enjoyed. It also stopped me celebrating anything that wasn't a complete success. It made me far more reserved, more inclined to stay quiet, and I would question every single thing I had done, and how it had come across to other people.

I had a really exposing conversation with Jamie when I was going through my pre-thirty panic, where he just said to me that he could not understand how I could look at everyone else and see the best in them and forgive them, and love them so wholeheartedly and yet not apply that same standard to myself. I couldn't embrace my failures because I couldn't trust myself to confront them and still love myself. I wasn't able to learn from my mistakes, because if I even started to contemplate them I would descend into self-loathing. The person I was afraid to make a fool of myself in front of, was me.

I needed to stop rewriting the narrative every time my life did not pan out exactly as I hoped, or as I felt those around me had hoped it would. I needed to be more realistic about the world around me, but I also needed to be more realistic about the world within me, my skills are sometimes also my worst flaw, for example my propensity to overthink things can be distinctly advantageous when it comes to planning, but it also means on occasions I end up with a warped view about the likelihood of negative things happening. Similarly, being able to identify with how other people might be feeling helps me stay motivated to try to do something to help, but that same insight can leave me overwhelmed to a point which renders me useless. Therefore, my mistakes ran alongside my successes and achievements. I used to say that anxiety felt like I was keeping a friend close, but an enemy closer. Being such an anxious person consistently pushed me outside of my comfort zone, and it actually made that a less scary place to be because I was already feeling constantly out of place. Yet, it also led me to magnify issues that shouldn't have been the problem they were. It made me agonise over painful memories and as a result of the fear of these arising again, it made me prone to panic.

I don't think anything happens in the simplified, perfect way we were taught to believe it does. I still want to get better, I want to be stronger physically and mentally, I want to keep challenging myself (part of that is the fact that I have now decided to tackle some of the emotional issues covered in this book head on, with professional help). I want to have aspirations and ambition, I want to keep striving to do better, and be better. I don't like having regrets, but I know they are important, and I must learn from them to move forward. I know, simply by the nature of who I am, that I won't feel this calm sense of understanding and acceptance all the time in the days and years to come. That I will still be afraid of entering domains where I don't fit. That I will still take too much on, and try and prove myself perfect for fear of rejection or of not doing justice to myself as a woman, and to women in general. That I will sometimes miss the little, happy moments as they happen, because I am blinded by a bigger issue at the time. That I will always want to be a bit better than the person I am, and I will always be slightly disappointed in myself. But I will continue to try, wholeheartedly to remember everything that not being the type has taught me, to accept me and the world around me as imperfect and glorious, and as a place where I belong.

The fear and panic of the first thirty years of my life have not disappeared. They remain an integral part of who I am, and of my story. They are what has finally taught me to take stock of the calmer, happier moments, even when these exist alongside sadness and failure. In truth, amongst that multitude of experiences I have talked about in this book there are so many moments that I wish I had understood as important. Standing in the sun, looking out over bright green rice fields in Cambodia. Drinking hot coffee and sucking mint sweets, standing around the campfire on a bitterly cold morning in Nagorno-Karabakh. Driving through the bush in Zimbabwe, with my headphones in. Laughing until I cried with my girlfriends as we reminisced about university.

They were as much the essence of my journey, as the difficult and the tragic, and they are the moments that have taught me some semblance of acceptance of the human condition. I truly do believe we can all make a difference, I think we must continue to challenge the idea that there is a right 'type' to do anything. A world that tells you what you are meant to be will sadly also never benefit from your full potential. And it's not just the world that's losing out in that scenario – it's you. It is terrifying when you feel like you don't fit in, I think so many of us know what that's like. To feel alone. To sit in that grey area and not know where to go. But within that grey area is opportunity, the opportunity to break barriers, to defy expectations, to be who you could be rather than who you should be.

I'm so glad and so lucky I didn't decide I was the 'wrong fit' for *Love Island* or for explosive ordnance disposal based on someone else's perception and interpretation of who I am. You can reinvent yourself, you can change, you can grow, you can regress, you can be any number of things at any particular time. Please give yourself permission to do that, and be equally as open-minded to others who choose. to do the same. Because perhaps, with just a little more compassion and acceptance, we won't need to fit in to feel that we belong.

The point is, the structures we have created as a society

have given the illusion of categories into which we must fall; professional, political, economic, social. But we exist beyond these, and this instinct to make sense of complex human nature, to categorise neatly, often means that there's little room for the complexities and the grey areas in between. I am not saying don't be interested and informed; in fact, I'm saying the opposite. Be interested. Be informed. Find out what you care about, because living a life defined by your passion is nothing short of extraordinary.

Postscript

Exclusive interview with Camilla for Audible Sessions, with Holly Newson

[voiceover] CAMILLA: _That was one of the hardest things to confront when I was writing the book, looking back at myself and just seeing that desperation for approval and then knowing that that's still part of me now._ [music]

HOLLY NEWSON: Camilla, lovely to have you here to chat about your new book _Not the Type_ . . . So for anyone who's watching this in a couple of months' time, or years' time, and they're wondering why we're sitting so far away, it's because we're just coming out of lockdown, not because we just, like . . . So to start with, I wondered if you could introduce us a bit to the book?

Not the Type

CAMILLA: It's basically about me trying to find my place in the real world . . . and struggling with feelings of not fitting in and of imposter syndrome, and yet finding that actually those experiences of feeling like an imposter have been some of the most important and formative in my life. And of course there's been ups and downs on that journey, but it's kind of helped me realise that we have to make sure that we consistently debunk stereotypes and myths about the best possible way for individuals to be, because they rarely serve the kind of multi-faceted people that we are. So that's the book.

HOLLY: And did you go into it thinking that you wanted to sort of put those things in, or did they come out as you wrote?

CAMILLA: So I went through quite a big process in the proposal side of things, where I kind of knew the themes and the narrative that I wanted the book to have. But I didn't anticipate how much would come out of the initial first draft process, and a big part of that is I was revisiting the first half of the book, which revisits my time with The HALO Trust. And as much as I think I remember everything it's funny, once you start writing, how much more starts to come out and kind of pours out of your memory, and it started unlocking things that I hadn't realised were there. So even though I had this really well-thought-out plan, actually writing the first draft I found myself having to incorporate new elements as I found them – as I discovered or rediscovered them.

Postscript

HOLLY: And you mentioned that when you joined The HALO Trust, what sort of inspired that decision to join something where you know you're going to be travelling, you're going to be out of your comfort zone, but I guess you're going to be helping people?

CAMILLA: Yeah – I mean, I'm lucky because The HALO Trust is very well known in Scotland, which is where I'm from, and actually their headquarters is quite close to where I grew up, so I'd been aware of them from when I was really young, and they were always kind of the ultimate job for me – they were like the dream job. I just couldn't see myself finding a way into it because I knew at that point – you know? – it was sort of predominantly ex-military men and they were incredibly skilled, and I just didn't know how I would ever get myself there. So I watched it from afar, thinking 'How can I find a way there?' but in the end it was that thing where I just had to apply, and I kind of thought maybe they'll say 'Come back in two years once you've done this or that.' That's what I was looking for in that first interview, for them to tell me what I needed to do, and I was just incredibly fortunate that I got that first role in Cambodia . . . because they were looking for it. At the time, for me, it was like this perfect collaboration of me working with these people that I aspired to be like, doing a job that I felt was worthwhile.

HOLLY: I'm really seeing the difference that it made. And yeah, right through that section [of the book]. So for anyone who's really curious about the sort of the details of landmines, and like how you take them apart, and also all sorts – you get that from the book. But you also write about the other side of fitting into that environment, and something that I could massively relate to, which was the constant one for approval, yeah? And I wondered, sort of, if you have a sense of where, for you, that comes from, and whether you have anything that you know in yourself now that means you're able to step back from wanting that approval all the time?

CAMILLA: I mean, that was one of the hardest things to confront when I was writing the book, looking back at myself and just seeing that desperation for approval and then knowing that that's still part of me now. I don't think my own voice was enough for me. I don't think I could listen to myself telling myself, 'You did a good job there,' or 'You're actually good at this.' I had to hear someone else say it, so at some point I must have devalued my own voice and then overvalued every single other person's, and so I was very guided by external voices. I think now I am a bit – a little bit – better at listening to my own voice but also talking back to my own voice. This is going to sound so weird, but yeah, now I question myself, because I have a very critical internal voice and I have definitely got better at questioning the voice that immediately tells me 'You're not good at this,' and trying to get reasons and answers. And trying to make myself a bit more resilient because it hampered my life being so . . . this desperate need for constant feedback and constant approval. I really would like to be at a stage where I can create that kind of sense of approval for myself, and also understand that – you know? – you can be doing something that everyone else is looking at thinking 'You know you're not doing that the best,' but if it means something to you and there's reasons why you're doing it, that is important. So I just . . . I'm trying now not to be so bound to that desperate need for approval and success in others' eyes, and look for internal validation of my choices.

HOLLY: So how much around mental health do you discuss in the book? What sort of things were important to you to put in there?

CAMILLA: In all honesty I think it [mental health] runs as a theme throughout the book, and I do have a specific chapter on anxiety. But I think for anyone reading the book, especially someone who does experience anxiety, you'll notice the signifiers of that, or you'll recognise maybe habits that can come up because of what anxiety creates within you as a person, of that desperate need for . . . control sometimes, or for that quiet sort of retreat from the world because it's less complicated to kind of turn in on yourself and to trap that kind of catastrophic thought cycle within yourself, rather than show it to the people around you. So I think for anyone reading the book, there'll be some who can see it all the way through. I suppose the other thing is touching on the . . . I touch on how mental health is discussed in the public domain, specifically on social media, because I have a very real worry we're flattening it as we put it into that kind of two-dimensional space. We're sort of saying 'Oh you can talk about mental health, but only when we understand it. You know, if you've got anxiety we can understand, when you're saying you're shy or you don't want to go and do this . . .' But if you talk about the genuine truly unpleasant symptoms of it, or of any mental health struggle, they're the ones that aren't seen as palatable in the public domain. And so the people who desperately need help the most, at the time when they need it the most, are the least likely to be able to speak of that . . . And so I do, I just have this genuine concern that we're starting to simplify that issue, and in doing so yes, we can say it's great that people feel more open about talking about their mental health issues now, you know? Certainly, for me, talking about anxiety has had huge benefits, and it's been amazing to see how people have responded to that. Equally, I worry about not finding the nuance in that space, and not enabling people who aren't experiencing anxiety the same way as me to talk about it as well.

HOLLY: You said that you know one way that anxiety can affect you is you wanting to sort of withdraw into yourself, and obviously you went completely the other way in going into *Love Island* and forcing yourself to have those social interactions. So how did you find yourself affected by that experience?

CAMILLA: Because so much of the reason why I went in was because I knew I was having this problem with socialising, and I knew that I needed to break down some of these walls that I had built up that I really did see as being for self-protection, but I could also see were severely affecting me in a negative way as well. And *Love Island* seemed like almost immersive kind of socialising. It was, like, as hard as it could have got for me at that point, and I have to say that experience . . . I mean, it worked in the way that I came out at the end and I felt so much closer to my friends and family again. And that was my main takeaway from that whole experience – like, that was the thing I was trying to get out of it.

HOLLY: And so that celebrity coming out of it – which I don't think anyone anticipated on the series that you were on because the show grew so much – how did you find that, adapting and also trying to build a relationship during that kind of constant gaze?

CAMILLA: Um . . . I think you just – you're almost allowed to be yourself, in a way, or to try and discover things about yourself, but then when you come out at the end that's when you can see all the [online] comments on what you've been doing for the last – for the previous few months. And that's maybe when the change happens and it becomes more complicated to understand what it feels like to have that – have those eyes on you and . . . Like you said, I really didn't anticipate – I didn't realise that it was going to get as big as it did that year, and that as many people were going to have, I guess, access to us afterwards, if that makes sense? Because everyone – I mean, that doesn't just stand for Love Islanders – everyone who's on social media now, people have access to you in a way that's difficult, and scrutinise you in a way that's difficult . . . I definitely wasn't prepared, and that was a difficult time that I cover in the book a bit as well.

HOLLY: When you came out of the villa, obviously you and Jamie hadn't been together for that long, so how did you sort of establish in such a new relationship what boundaries you were going to have, in terms of what you wanted to share and what you wanted to keep to yourselves, and things like that?

CAMILLA: I mean, I think we always were kind of on the same page with that – it never really was a big discussion between us. But also, in a way we were fortunate with the timing, like you meet . . . we met a couple of weeks before the show ended so we did get to meet on the show. I don't think I'd have met him in any other walk of life, you know? We had very different jobs, um, so that was incredibly fortunate. But then the timing was quite nice, because then, when we really did want to get to know each other, it was outside of being on the show and we could meet each other's families and each other's friends and just see whether our lives did overlap.

HOLLY: Is there any one takeaway or, like, the biggest takeaway, that you hope people will get from the book?

CAMILLA: That even when it feels like you're very alone – when it feels like you're doing everything wrong, that every decision you make is wrong, that no one can understand what you can see in your own head as being the life you want to lead. That [other people's] concept of what you should be doing is just a mirage, just a structure that we have created through various different sorts of societal structures – you know, economic, professional, political, those places don't actually exist – so even when you think you're fitting into the right place you're going to feel so out of place anyway because it's not a real thing. So it's much better to spend some time going through those failures, going through those bad decisions, really getting to know yourself, really understanding yourself and letting yourself be a contradictory person to find out who you really are. And be really open to change as well – that's the other thing, that you don't have to be the same person tomorrow as you were today. That can feel lonely, but it's something we all experience, so you're not alone.

HOLLY: Well, thank you so much – it's been an absolute pleasure to chat to you.

CAMILLA: Thank you so much.

Interview reproduced, with grateful thanks, by permission of Audible UK.

Glossary

AVR   armed violence reduction

AXO   abandoned explosive ordnance is explosive ordnance that has not been used during armed conflict and has been left behind, and is no longer under control of the party that abandoned it

DRC   Danish Refugee Council

EOD   explosive ordnance disposal

ERW   explosive remnants of war are explosive munitions left behind after a conflict has ended. ERW consists of unexploded ordnance (UXO) and abandoned explosive ordnance (AXO)

FCO   Foreign and Commonwealth Office

FFE   free from explosives

GPR   ground-penetrating radar

HALO   'Hazardous Area Life-support Organisation'. How The HALO Trust got its name, although it is now rarely referred to as that. See: https://www.halotrust.org/

HOBB   high-order burning box, used to destroy landmines by heating them until they detonate

HSTAMIDS handheld standoff mine detection system, a mine detector that combines an electromagnetic induction sensor, ground-penetrating radar (GPR), and sophisticated algorithms to detect landmines while rejecting most clutter

IDP   internally displaced person; people who are refugees within their own countries

IMAS   International Mine Action Standards, the standards applied in all UN mine-action operations

ISIL   Islamic State of Iraq and the Levant; also referred to as IS

MRE   mine-risk education

Glossary

NGO   non-governmental organisation; a (usually) not-for-profit organisation that operates independently of any government, typically in the fields of humanitarian and social issues

NVESD   Night Vision and Electronic Sensors Directorate, a unit of the US Army

OCD   obsessive-compulsive disorder

OSCE   Organisation for Security and Cooperation in Europe; see note 4, page 46

Peshmerga   the military forces of the autonomous Kurdistan Region of Iraq; they played a significant part in the defeat of IS

PPE   personal protective equipment

SOP   standard operating procedure

UEMS   unplanned explosions at munition sites

UNHCR   United Nations High Commission for Refugees, the UN's refugee agency, established in 1950

UXO   unexploded ordnance refers to weapons that failed to detonate as intended. These unstable explosive devices are left behind during and after conflicts and pose dangers similar to landmines

WASH	water, sanitation and hygiene
Yazidi	the Yazidis are an ethnic and religious minority indigenous to Turkey, Syria and, principally, Iraq. Forced to flee by ISIL attacks on Iraqi cities in 2014, many were murdered, and thousands enslaved, especially women and children

Acknowledgements

Thank you to Toby Buchan, my editor, who from the moment we met, spoke with such clarity about the theme of the typescript and had such faith in my writing skills that it almost felt as if the book materialised before my eyes. As the first person to give me feedback on my writing in over ten years, it was a near-impossible task and I am so grateful for both your skills as an editor, but also your ability to deliver notes with wit and humour.

Thank you to the entire team at Metro Publishing and Bonnier Books. I will never look at a book again without thinking about how many talented people contribute to its creation, and I am so grateful to you all for your hard work and support.

Thank you to my agent Jadeen Singh, for being as kind as you are talented, and for always treating me with that kindness. Thank you for everything you have done for me over the last few years, but in particular for going above and beyond to instil me with confidence in the book, and in my life.

Thank you to my literary agent Ben Dunn, who has been instrumental, at every stage of the process, in turning the book into a reality.

Thank you to The HALO Trust. My life was significantly changed for the better because you gave me a chance. But thank you, too, for your continued commitment to incredibly difficult work in dangerous places, in order to make the world a safer place.

Thank you to all the team at *Love Island*. You also changed my life in a way I could have never imagined. Thank you all for being more than a team behind a show, but being true friends to me both then and now.

Thank you to all my wonderful friends, who have put up with a lot over the years. I don't know how you do it but I am eternally grateful that you do, and I love you. Particular thanks to Emily Haigh, Cassie Anne Shaw (née Worman), Jessica Williams, Stephanie Daniels (née Eayrs), Stefanie Allen, Bessie Deakin, Maryanna Baston, Catherine Ainsworth, Katherine Douglas, Nina Hurel and Natalie Allan.

Thank you to my dogs Audrey and Gus. I treasure the memories of you sitting quietly beside me in your bed while I was writing (and less so the ones of you barking wildly at the postwoman, the backdoor creaking, the leaves drifting by the window and any other slight noise while I was trying to write). You have done a magnificent job of guarding Jamie and me from absolutely nothing, but I adore how

Acknowledgements

protective you are of us and we couldn't love you any more than we do.

Thank you to Jamie for your endless support, for your willingness to walk the dogs alone and for only occasionally surreptitiously watching boxing videos on your phone while pretending to listen to my worries about the book. You know and I know that I could not have done this without you – I love you.

Thank you to my family. Thank you, Mum, for constantly reminding all your children to eat and sleep, and for somehow always messaging us at exactly the right moment to say exactly the right thing. Thank you, Dad, for always being ridiculously enthusiastic about all of your children's projects and for believing we can do just about anything. Thank you to my brother and sisters for being supportive in the manner that only siblings can be, and in doing so making sure I believed in myself, while still keeping my feet firmly on the ground. I am exceptionally lucky to have you as my family, and I love you.